The
Heart of
the Gospel

The Heart of the Gospel

Martyn Lloyd Jones

Edited by
Christopher Catherwood

CROSSWAY BOOKS
EASTBOURNE

ISBN 1 85684 000 X

Production and Printing in England for
C R O S S W A Y   B O O K S
Glyndley Manor, Pevensey, Eastbourne, East Sussex BN24 5BS by
Nuprint Ltd, Station Road, Harpenden, Herts AL5 4SE

CONTENTS

FOREWORD

I remember it as if it were yesterday, though in fact it was an evening in 1948, when I was a Christian four years old in the faith. I had been told that this man and his ministry were in a class by themselves, and was trying to imagine what might be special about them. My friend led me straight to a front pew a little left of centre at the back of a great tiered gallery that ran all round the building; he told me it was the best place to see from, and seeing was important. I looked around. Westminster Chapel was a big, high, gloomy, lozenge-shaped Victorian structure seating three thousand, a thousand downstairs and in each of the two galleries. Huge organ pipes rose up behind the pulpit, and the pulpit itself, the focal point for the eye, had been built as a large circular platform, drawing-room size, some distance off the ground (though below the level of the first gallery), with steps leading up to it on either side. Spurgeon's Tabernacle had evidently been the architect's model here. The decor was dark-coloured, and the building was not well lit.

The preacher was a small man with a big head and evidently thinning hair, wearing a shapeless-looking black gown. His great domed forehead caught the eye at once. He walked briskly to the little pulpit desk in the centre of the balcony, said 'Let us pray' in a rather pinched, deep, Welsh-inflected, microphone-magnified voice, and at once began pleading with God to visit us during the service. The blend of reverence and intimacy, adoration and dependence, fluency and simplicity in his praying was remarkable: he had a great gift in prayer. Soon he was reading a Bible chapter (Matthew 11), briskly and intelligently rather than dramatically or weightily; and in due course the auditorium lights went out and he launched into a 45-minute sermon on history, and the story of God's kingdom as the centre of history, and the crucial place of John the Baptist in that story, as forerunner of the Saviour-King who is at the centre of the centre, Jesus Christ the Lord. The sermon (as we say nowadays) blew me away.

What was special about it? It was simple, clear, straightforward man-to-man stuff. It was expository, apologetic, and evangelistic on the grand scale. It was both the planned performance of a magnetic orator and the passionate, compassionate outflow of a man with a message from God that he knew his hearers needed. He worked up to a dramatic growling shout about God's sovereign grace a few minutes before the end; then from that he worked down to businesslike persuasion, calling on needy souls to come to Christ. It was the old, old story, but it had been made wonderfully new. I went out full of awe and joy, with a more vivid sense of the greatness of God in my heart than I had known before.

During the winter, 1948–49, Dr. Lloyd-Jones preached through the whole of Matthew 11, delivering the sermons that make up this book. The thunder and lightning; the gestures—kneading fists representing perplexed philosophers, the vibrating arm with open hand marking God's descent in grace, the right-angled turns to point to heaven and hell (one side of the church for each, and always the same side); and the electric impact of those trombone-sforzando shouts about God—these are elements which only readers who, like me, heard the sermons can supply. But if any reader fails to find in these messages as majestic an exposition of the everlasting gospel as he, or she, has ever met, I shall—to put it mildly—

be surprised. They impress me as among the ripest fruit of the greatest period of a great man's ministry, and it is a privilege as well as a pleasure to be introducing them now, after forty years locked up in a shorthand transcript, to a new generation.

J.I. Packer

1

The Vital Question

Now when John had heard in the prison the works of Christ, he sent two of his disciples, And said unto him, Art thou he that should come, or do we look for another? Jesus answered and said unto them, Go and shew John again those things which ye do hear and see: The blind receive their sight, and the lame walk, the lepers are cleansed, and the deaf hear, the dead.are raised up, and the poor have the gospel preached to them. And blessed is he, whosoever shall not be offended in me (MATTHEW 11:2–6).

These words bring us directly face to face with the great central theme of the New Testament. John the Baptist, bound in prison, sent his two disciples to put this famous question to Jesus of Nazareth: 'Art thou He that should come, or do we look for another?' In other words, the question was, 'Are you the Messiah whom we have been expecting, or are we mistaken, those of us who believe that you are; and must we start looking for someone else or wait for the Messiah to come?' So this is the crucial question which is put, in some shape or form, everywhere in the New Testament: 'Art thou He that should come?'; 'What think ye of Christ, whose Son is He?' The four Gospels are all portraits of this person; they present Him to us and hold Him before us.

Look too at the Acts of the Apostles and you will find that the first preachers, under the auspices of the Christian Church, went round and preached and talked about Jesus, the same person. Then go on to the Epistles and you will find that they are full of this name; every book of the New Testament is calling attention to Him.

So then, we are obviously, here, dealing with this great theme. Christianity, we are reminded, is essentially something that concerns the person of the Lord Jesus Christ. We start with that fact and emphasise it, because Christianity is not primarily a teaching, nor a philosophy, nor even a way of life. In the first instance it is, before all, a relationship to a person. The New Testament in a sense, will not even discuss with us the kind of life we are going to live until we have come to a satisfactory answer about Him. All along, it shuts us down to this one matter and holds us up against this one thing; it refuses to discuss our questions and our problems with us except in terms of this person. 'I want to live a good life,' says someone. 'All right,' replies the New Testament, 'but before we can discuss with you how you can live such a life, what have you made of Him? Where does He come into your scheme of things? What is His place and position in your whole outlook and world?'

Now that, let me emphasise again, is something that is really vital and central. The whole message of the New Testament is to say certain things about Him, everything it has to say is in terms of Him. It starts with Him; it is the gospel of Jesus Christ. It makes the amazing claim for Him that He was none other than the Son of God come down into this world. It tells us that He and He alone is the Saviour of the world, that He came into the world in order to save it and that there is no heaven apart from Him.

Then, having made this great claim, the New Testament goes on to say that the most important question, therefore, which we must face is that of Jesus Christ; for, it tells us, our life in this world here and now, the whole meaning of death, and, indeed, our life throughout eternity, depends entirely

and solely upon our answer to this question: 'Art thou He
that should come or do we look for another?' The New
Testament does not hesitate to say that. Listen to the Apostle
Peter saying it unequivocally in one of his first recorded
sermons: 'There is none other name under heaven given
among men whereby we must be saved' (Acts 4:12)—this
name of the Lord Jesus Christ.

Now that is a dogmatic assertion, I agree, but there is a
no more dogmatic book in the world than the New Testament. It never comes and says, 'You have read many other
books and been interested in their theories, now read me and
see what you make of me. Perhaps you will find me more
interesting than the others.' No, rather, it makes a definite
pronouncement. Here, it tells us, is the only way for men and
women to know God and to be reconciled to him. Here is the
only way in which they can be delivered from the thraldom
and the serfdom of life in this world, and from its sin and its
evil. Here is the only way whereby they can be delivered for
ever from the fear of death and the grave. And here, says the
New Testament, is the one and only way in which men and
women can avoid spending eternity in a state of misery and
wretchedness and torment. That is its statement, nothing less.
'He that believeth on the Son hath everlasting life; and he that
believeth not the Son shall not see life; but the wrath of God
abideth upon him' (Jn 3:36). It is one or the other; everything
is dependent upon this person.

So I think I have demonstrated that whatever you may
think of the New Testament message, it is the person who
comes first; not religion or a good life. Indeed, the New
Testament comes to us and says, 'I am not interested in your
views about anything until we are clear about your views
about him.' He is central, he is first, and if we are wrong about
him, it does not make any difference, even if we are right
everywhere else.

Therefore, in the light of this message, there is nothing of
such vital importance to us as just this question: What is Jesus
Christ to us? John, there in prison, sent his two messengers

because he had realised that it was the most important question on earth and in life: is this the Messiah, or is it not? Now I do not want to detract in any way from the large number of questions that are engaging people's attention at the present time. They are perfectly legitimate and we should be concerned about them. The New Testament does not tell us, while we are in this world, that we are not to be concerned, for example, as to whether there is to be war or not. Certainly these things are important, and we all have to live, and there are other interests which are equally legitimate. But it does say that all these things are merely passing. There may be a war, or there may not; all these things may or may not happen, we do not know. 'In any case,' says the New Testament, 'your life in this world is just passing, but here is something that will always be of concern, something which will follow you beyond this world; it affects your whole everlasting and eternal destiny—how tremendously important it is!'

Our Lord presented himself to the people in these terms, and his followers went round the world preaching it in the same way. We have a record of it here, but we also see here the response which that message had. The New Testament always tells us how people reacted to it. Fortunately for us, it not only makes its positive statements, it records history at the same time and it tells us quite plainly that there were many people who rejected this message. Some did not even listen, others thought about it and almost believed, then did not; there were all sorts of varying reactions. So I thank God for this record, because many of us have often seen ourselves in some of these historical pictures of the New Testament. The glory of the record is that it puts our case in a very much better way than we could ever put it ourselves.

Now here in this incident we have one example and illustration of a difficulty with respect to Jesus Christ. It is the famous case of John the Baptist, and we shall make use of this incident, as it affects so many today. There is light here upon the problems that affect some people in exactly the same way as they did John the Baptist and his followers. Let me just give you the picture so that we may understand the background.

John the Baptist, let me remind you, had borne very striking testimony to this person before the incident that we are considering here. One day he was standing with some of his own followers when he saw Jesus of Nazareth, walking along; and he turned to his men and said, 'Behold the Lamb of God that taketh away the sin of the world.' John had there made this mighty statement, that this person was none other than the Messiah. John, a Jew, like all other Jews, was looking forward to the coming of a great deliverer. That was the great hope that kept the children of Israel going through the many vicissitudes of their strange life. They had the promise, which had been given to them by God through his various servants, that a Messiah, an unusual, extraordinary person, would come. Isaiah 35 is one example of that, and of the blessings that would follow when this deliverer came. So the people were longing for His coming. Now John had borne testimony that Jesus Christ was the one for whom they were looking: 'There He is,' said John, 'behold the Lamb of God.'

But now John is in prison, where he has been for some time, and from there he sends his two followers with this question. Is this a doubt? No, I do not think so. This is depression and there is all the difference in the world between doubt and depression in a believer. I do not want to stay with that, but we must hold on to the vital difference between these two things. John, probably because of the physical conditions of prison, was depressed. I have no doubt also, but that this was greatly encouraged by his own followers. There was possibly a certain amount of jealous feeling regarding Jesus Christ who was gathering a greater crowd to Him, and the followers of John were a little concerned about this. They were probably reminding John of that in prison and saying to him, 'John, if this is the Messiah, why does he allow you to stay in prison? Wouldn't he deliver you if he was the Messiah?' So John had been hearing all this, and he was tired and, in all likelihood, suffering physically, and in this state of depression he sends his question.

There has always been a great argument as to whether

John was saying this for himself or on behalf of his disciples, but in a sense it does not matter at all. I am prepared to agree with either or both suggestions. It may have been a sort of omnibus question, as if John turned to his disciples and said, 'Well, after all, there seems to be something in what you are saying. Let us ask him, "Art thou He that should come or do we look for another?" Give us the answer,' said John to our Lord, 'it is vital to us. Are we to pin our faith entirely on you, or are we to wait and expect someone else? Are you the one I said you were; are you the one you claim to be?'

Here, therefore, is a picture which tells us a story and reminds us that as far as this person of the message is concerned, people in this world have difficulties about it. Indeed, our Lord draws attention to it in the last statement. 'This is my final word,' he says to John's followers. 'Go back and say this: "Blessed is he whosoever shall not be offended in me."' This means 'Happy is the man who does not find a source of offence in me; blessed is the man who does not stumble at me, and who lets nothing stand between him and a true belief in me.'

Now there are various things that cause people to stumble. There are many accounts of this in the pages of the Gospels and in the Acts of the Apostles and there are many subsequent records in the Christian Church. There are people who stumble at Christ and His message, and it is in order that I may try to meet some of their difficulties that I call attention to this subject. My reason for doing this is not because I am merely interested in the New Testament and its teaching. No, it is rather because if this is right, not to believe is damnation; if this is right, it is the most urgent problem in the world today, and it is the thing that decides my soul's eternal salvation. So, then, let us look at it.

There are those who do not even consider Him, they never think about Him at all. We need not stay with them—if there is any such person reading this then I ask you to think again and to consider Him immediately. But I am concerned rather with those who have looked at Him and are conscious of certain difficulties. Let us try to help their needs as we work out this incident together. Indeed, we shall go on to consider a number of the difficulties about Him, because you will find in this one chapter of Matthew most of the difficulties that people find today with respect to a belief in the Lord Jesus Christ. We can classify them like this. First, there are problems with respect to His person; secondly, people have trouble with respect to what happened to Him, and thirdly, there are difficulties with respect to what He did and did not do.

Now all are suggested in this one incident, and so let us begin by dealing with the problems with regard to the person of Jesus Christ. Let me put them plainly and simply and directly. Who is and what is this Jesus of Nazareth? Is He only man or is He more than that; is He just a great teacher on the moral situation; is He but the greatest of all philosophers, a supreme thinker? What are the claims that are made for Him? These are the things at which many people stumble.

'Yes,' says someone, 'I am interested in Jesus of Nazareth. I like reading about Him, I am interested in His teaching and I want to live the life He lived. But the New Testament does not stop at that, it goes on to talk about the miracle of the incarnation, it asks me to believe that the baby lying in the manger in Bethlehem was that eternal Son of God who existed in the bosom of the Father from all eternity but who had become and was made flesh and entered into the life of this world. It says that He came out of eternity into time— the miracle of the incarnation—God taking upon himself the human form and becoming man. That is my problem,' says this person, 'the incarnation, which your New Testament and the dogmatic teaching of the Christian Church ask me to accept.'

'Then,' he says, 'there is the whole claim about the virgin birth. I am asked to believe that He was born of a virgin; that He was conceived of the Holy Spirit; that, unlike every child born into this world, He did not have a human father, though He had a human mother, and that the Holy Spirit came upon

her and overshadowed her, and that of the Holy Spirit she
bore a son. I am in trouble over that too.

'And then the New Testament asks you to believe this
extraordinary doctrine about His person; to believe that He
had two natures and yet there was only one person. It asks us
to believe that in Him was both the divine nature and the
human nature; not an intermingling of the human and divine;
two natures but only one person; truly human, truly divine
yet one being. You ask us to believe that He is God and
man—God-man.

'Now,' says the questioner, 'there is my trouble, my
problem. Jesus? Yes, all right. The teaching? Fine, one of the
best the world has ever seen—would that the whole world
were practising it! I am prepared to walk after Him and to try
to imitate and follow His example, but your gospel goes
further than that. I am asked to believe these other things and
I cannot. I cannot grasp this idea of the incarnation, this
miracle. Life is not like that, there are no miracles in real life. I
am accustomed to see things which I can touch and feel and
measure and handle, things that are amenable to my understanding and which my mind and reason and logic can grasp.
But here you are introducing all these supernatural things
which I cannot accept.'

There are many today who stumble at these things; they
cannot grasp them or believe them. They are doubtful and
uncertain about it all, but they cannot leave it. They have
attended the preaching of the Church, they have listened to
sermons about Jesus Christ, they are reading books about
Him and yet they know they are not Christians. They are
unhappy in the world face to face with these problems, they
cannot leave them alone and yet they cannot submit and
believe on Him; they stumble at the doctrine concerning His
person.

Now what do we say to them? Well, fortunately, the
answer to such people is given in a very clear and explicit
manner in this famous story. What the New Testament says
to every such person can be put like this: 'My friend, if that is

your position—and I understand it and sympathise with it and I want to deal with it as lovingly and as sympathetically as I can—then the great message for you from the incident which we are considering is this: go to Him, go at once to Him and send your message to Him.'

Let me put it negatively. These great matters which we have been mentioning are not issues for abstract or philosophical discussion or consideration. They are not subjects that are put only in the realm of reasoning. Now that is the lesson of John the Baptist. There he is in the prison, surrounded by his followers, and they are asking him, 'Do you think you are right? We hear that He is doing some things and not doing others, and, in any case, why does He leave you here in prison?' And so the argument goes on. Then John does the right thing; he says in effect, 'No more debate and discussion, just go to Him.' And he sends two of his disciples to say to Him, 'Art thou He that should come, or look we for another.' I suggest, therefore, that the solution to this particular difficulty is that we must realise at the very outset that if we deal with it solely in an abstract, academic, philosophical manner, we shall never solve it or understand it.

There are good reasons for that. Let me give you but two. First—and surely this is one that ought to be sufficient in and of itself—if what the Bible tells us about him is right and true, then, of necessity, it is something which transcends human intellect and reason. 'Quite right,' you say, 'I cannot understand the miracles.' Of course you cannot, no one can understand a miracle, it would cease to be a miracle if you could. 'I cannot grasp the supernatural.' Most certainly you cannot, there never has been a man who could understand the doctrine of the incarnation. I think of the incarnation, and I take up my stand on the side of the Apostle Paul who said, 'Great is the mystery of godliness' (1 Tim 3:16). My mind is too small to understand it, my intellect cannot span the infinities and the immensities and the eternities. My little pigmy reason and logic are not big enough to see or to take in such a conception as the self-emptying and the humiliation of the Son of God. I do not claim to understand it; who could understand an idea like that of the virgin birth? It is beyond understanding, it is beyond reason. Who can understand the doctrine of the two natures, unmixed, remaining separate, unmingled and yet both there, but still only one person? I cannot understand the doctrine of the Trinity, Father Son and Holy Spirit. I cannot, and we should never try to do so.

The claim of the gospel is that it is in a realm which is beyond human reasoning and understanding. It is a revelation, a statement that comes to us, an announcement; it is the gift of God. That is why instead of reasoning round and round in circles and trying to span and grasp the infinite and the everlasting, I say, go to Him!

The second reason is that if it were a matter of understanding and abstract reasoning, then this gospel of the New Testament and salvation would just be for a handful of people in this world. You would have to be an expert philosopher; you would have to start with an unusual brain, and then you would have to go to colleges and universities to be trained in philosophy. So there would be no gospel for the common, ordinary man. But, thank God, here is a gospel which tells us that 'the common people heard Him gladly' (Mk 12:37). Philosophers cannot preach to the poor; the poor could not follow them, and all the Greek philosophers have nothing to say to such people. But the gospel is preached to the poor. Here, then, is a proof of the whole thing. It is not understanding that is essential, it is accepting, and submitting; it is giving yourself to Jesus Christ.

So we see that the message of the gospel is that if you are in trouble and in difficulty about Him, don't stop there arguing and going round in circles. I say this with feeling because I have known myself what that means. I did it for years, arguing and reasoning, and you come back exactly to where you began. I do not hesitate to say that if you persist in trying to understand the essence of this gospel you will die in the same position as you are now, you will never do it. Do what John the Baptist did, go to Him, as you see Him in the Gospels.

That is why, by the grace of God, the Gospels have been written. We cannot go in the flesh but we can go to the Gospels and have a look at Him. And this is what we see. We are struck at once by the strange paradoxical element; we are impressed by the apparent contradiction. We look and say, 'Isn't He remarkably like us?' and the next minute we say, 'How absolutely different!' It is this curious contradiction. Take His great claim for Himself—'Before Abraham was, I am' (Jn 8:58). 'He that hath seen me hath seen the Father' (Jn 14:9). 'I am the way, the truth and the life; no man cometh unto the Father but by me' (Jn 14:6). 'Ye have heard that it was said by them of old time ... but I say unto you' (Mt 5:27–28). What an astounding claim he makes for Himself and His own person. Then listen, too, to the extraordinary claims He makes upon other people. There is a man sitting at the receipt of custom, following his job as usual, then this person comes along and says, 'Follow me! Leave everything!' He demands a totalitarian allegiance: what a claim for a man to make for himself and of other people!

And then look at Him again and behold His understanding. Listen to Him as He expounds the Scriptures in a way no one ever did before. He knows more than the doctors of the law, there is an authority in His speech which man has never known before. Then look at His works, His miracles of healing; look at Him walking upon the sea, look at this astounding man and His works of power. Look at His sinlessness—no one can point a finger at Him, He is absolutely sinless and perfect.

Then there is another side which is extraordinary. How has He attained all this knowledge and information? Can you explain it in terms of birth and upbringing? His so-called parents were so poor that there was no room for them in the inn when He was born and He was born in a stable. They could not offer anything better than two turtle doves when He was presented in the Temple. He was a carpenter, and had no training like the Pharisees. He never went to the schools; so you cannot explain it in terms of His human birth or

natural upbringing and surroundings. And yet He had knowledge; it was admitted by his enemies.

Then, in contrast with this amazing power and authority
and assurance concerning Himself, look at His lowliness—'a
bruised reed shall He not break and the smoking flax shall He
not quench' (Is 42:3)—the meek and lowly Jesus. There was
never such a person as this. He could command the storm and
quell the raging of the waves of the sea. He was full of
sympathy and compassion; He was a friend of publicans and
sinners. He knew what it was to be tired and to be hungry and
weary. Though He could command the elements, He suffered
these things; though He knew so much, He said at certain
points that there were certain things He did not know. He
said that all his teaching was given to Him by God His Father.
When He had an important matter, such as the choosing of
His disciples, He got up a great while before day and prayed
to God. 'I am dependent,' He said, 'upon Him.'

So there He is, knowing everything, yet not knowing
certain things; this curious mixture, this strange enigma, these
apparent contradictions in this person. Are you in trouble
about Him? Then, rush to Him, go to Him in the Gospels.
Furthermore, don't stop at that. If you are in trouble about
the incarnation and the virgin birth and His person and all
these things, not only go to Him there, get on your knees also.
Speak to Him, tell Him about your trouble, ask Him for the
Holy Spirit, ask Him for light. Say, 'I cannot leave you alone,
I am not satisfied, I am stumbling at these things, enlighten
my darkness, satisfy my demands.' Go to Him like that, and,
as you do so, I think you will get an answer similar to that
which John had.

There are also certain great answers given to these difficulties in the New Testament. The first is this vital matter of
the fulfilment of prophecy. Look again at what our Lord said
to John's disciples: 'Go and shew John again those things
which ye do hear and see: the blind receive their sight, and the
lame walk, the lepers are cleansed, and the deaf hear, the dead
are raised up, and the poor have the gospel preached to them.'

Why did He say that? He did so because the prophets of old had said that when the Messiah came, He would do that kind of thing. 'Go back and tell John,' said our Lord, 'that I am doing the very things which the prophets prophesied concerning the Messiah.' So if you are in trouble about the person of Christ, read the Old Testament prophecies. You will find that His birth was predicted—it is all there in amazing detail. 'We have the word of prophecy made more sure,' says Peter. Make a list of all the things that are said about this Messiah and see how they are all verified in Him.

Then, of course, the New Testament goes on to tell us something that our Lord did not say here to John the Baptist. If you are in trouble about this person, look at the mighty fact of the resurrection, because there would not have been a Christian Church at all were it not that He rose from the dead. You have to cater for the resurrection, you must explain it somehow. Furthermore, consider all the things He has done down the running centuries of time. Look what He did to His followers and disciples, and at what He has done ever since. Read the story of the Christian Church: can you explain it apart from what we are told of Him in the Bible? It is the greatest force the world has ever known. Human history would never have been written apart from Him—you cannot explain or understand it. He dominates everything; even through that Cross of His, he 'towers o'er the wrecks of time'.

So the great lesson and message is that if we have these problems and difficulties, we must stop trying to understand. We must give up reasoning and arguing and go back and face Him. Look at Him, look at Him in the Bible, speak to Him in prayer, consider this subsequent testimony of the Christian Church and if you do, I suggest that you are bound to come to the conclusion which many another has come to before you. We read in John chapter 7 about certain officers who were sent to apprehend our Lord. The authorities, who were displeased with Christ and could not make Him out at all, sent these men to arrest Him and to bring Him before them. But after a while they came back without Christ. 'What is the

matter?' they were asked. 'Why don't you produce the prisoner?' And the officers' reply was, 'Never man spake like this
man,' or in other words: 'Gentlemen,' said the officers, 'you
are sitting here in Jerusalem, arguing and talking about a man
and you cannot understand and make out who he is. And
while we listened to your discussion we felt as you did, but
you sent us to arrest him so we went and began to listen to
what he had to say and "never man spake like this man". We
do not understand him but we cannot touch him. In fact if
you, too, stopped arguing and listened to him you would
begin to realise why no one ever spoke as he did.' You see
their trouble was solved by going to Christ.

And then there was another soldier, the Centurion. He,
too, had heard all the discussions about this extraordinary
person who claimed He was the Messiah and then he had just
seen him crucified in apparent weakness. And as he looked at
him dying and expiring, this was his comment: 'Surely this
man was the Son of God' (Mk 15:39).

My last example is none other than the disciple, the
Apostle Thomas, and what a perfect illustration he is of this
very thing. You see, my point is that as long as you just reason
and argue and go round and round in circles, you will never
be satisfied, but the moment you see Him your troubles will
be resolved and your answers will be given to you. Here is the
story of Thomas. After the death of Christ, the Apostles were
scattered. Then they met together, and, when they were in an
upper room, Christ appeared to them. Thomas was not with
them then but he joined the company later. They told him
that the Lord had appeared among them, but Thomas would
not believe it. He kept to the realm of reason and understanding. 'No,' he said, 'I can't believe it, I cannot accept it, I must
see Him for myself. I must put my hand into the print of the
nails; I cannot believe this story.' But then later the Lord
appeared in the room and said, 'Where is that finger of yours
Thomas? Put it into my side.' And Thomas broke down, as it
were, and said that it was unnecessary. He fell at His feet and
said, 'My Lord and my God.' Had he come to understand the

resurrection? Of course he had not, he just knew that it was a fact.

So it is not a question of understanding, it is a question of the facts. Here they are confronting us, this amazing person, appearing as God only, as man only and yet clearly both. Can you explain Him in any other terms? Is there anything else that one can really do but to join these people and say, 'God-man, God the Son come in the flesh, my Lord and my God?' My friends, give up this futile attempt to understand the illimitable and the absolute and go to Him and look at Him in the Bible. Speak to Him in prayer, ask Him, apply to Him, go straight to headquarters. Go to Him, Himself, and leave it all to Him and He will give you an answer which, if you are honest, will satisfy your soul and save it for time and for eternity. 'Art thou He that should come or look we for another?' He is the Lord Jesus Christ, the Son of God, the Saviour of the world.

2

Go To Christ

Now when John had heard in the prison the works of Christ, he sent two of his disciples, And said unto Him, Art thou he that should come, or do we look for another? Jesus answered and said unto them, Go and shew John again those things which ye do hear and see: The blind receive their sight, and the lame walk, the lepers are cleansed, and the deaf hear, the dead are raised up, and the poor have the gospel preached to them. And blessed is he, whosoever shall not be offended in me (MATTHEW 11:2–6).

As we have seen, we are confronted in these verses with the central theme and message of the New Testament, which is to bring us all face to face with the Lord Jesus Christ. The New Testament does not bring us a general message about peace and war and culture and education. No, first and foremost it tells us about this person.

Furthermore, it claims that He is the Messiah, the Saviour of the world. It says that there has never been anyone like Him in this world, that He is the Son of God made flesh dwelling among us as man—God-man. It also tells us that we must not compare Him with all the great teachers the world has known, whether philosophers or religious teachers in a special sense; we must not compare Him with Confucius,

Buddha, Mohammed and so on, because he is different, in a category apart. The New Testament claim, in other words, is that here we have an account of what God himself has done about men and women and about the world. It is about God's way of salvation and its great message is to ask us to face that; that is its concern, everywhere.

Now we have been considering this account of John the Baptist because it not only confronts us with that question, but because it does, at the same time, remind us of the difficulties which different people seem to find with regard to this all-important matter. John, let me remind you, was in prison and, while not doubting, was discouraged. His disciples were full of doubt as to whether our Lord was the Messiah or not, so John sent them immediately to Christ Himself to ask if He really was 'He that should come'. And you remember how our Lord sent back a message and reminded John of what he had seen and heard, and then He added the footnote: 'Blessed is he whosoever shall not be offended in Me'—Blessed is the man who does not find something in Me that offends him. Blessed is he who does not put an obstacle between himself and belief in Me.

There are, therefore, we are reminded here, certain things at which people seem to stumble. They read the New Testament and hear a presentation of its message and then they say, 'Yes—but...'! As we have seen, there are at any rate three main causes for this 'but'. We have looked at the problems and difficulties about the person of Christ—the incarnation, the virgin birth, the problems about the doctrine of two natures in one person and the difficulty about the great doctrine of the Trinity.

I also indicated that there was a second problem, which is the difficulty about the things that happened to Him, especially His death. And the third difficulty is the problem of what He did and did not do.

So let us now consider the second difficulty. There are so many people who stumble at this New Testament doctrine about the death of Christ. I suppose there is a sense in which it is true to say that this is a greater cause of stumbling than any other—the doctrine of the cross; the bread and the wine and what they represent, and the blood of Christ. This has always been a difficulty; it was a difficulty even to the disciples themselves. When our Lord spoke to them at Caesarea Philippi and began to talk to them explicitly about His death, even Peter, who had just said, 'Thou art the Christ the Son of the living God', even he said, 'Be it far from thee Lord'—that must not happen to you; and they had to be rebuked. They all stumbled at the cross, they could not understand it. They all forsook him and fled, and it was only after his resurrection that they truly came to understand it. You find in exactly the same way that it was a great stumbling block to the people to whom the gospel was first preached—'the preaching of the cross is to them that perish foolishness' (1 Cor 1:18)—and people have been troubled about this throughout the ages. They find it difficult to believe, and it is the one thing that has stood between them and a belief in Him.

So let us be clear about this, and consider first what the New Testament says about it. On this subject, there can be no question at all. According to the New Testament, the cross, the death of Christ, is not only vital, it is absolutely central. You will find this in the teaching of our Lord himself (I will refer to that later). Then look at the preaching of the Apostles as it is recorded in the Book of Acts and you will find that all along they went around and preached about his death—how the Christ must suffer—and about the meaning of that death upon the cross. Peter's first sermon on the day of Pentecost was really nothing but an exposition of that. Paul, too, gives us a very graphic picture in writing to the Galatians, saying that he *placarded* the death on the cross. He is like a man holding up a placard and on it is the cross. 'I determined,' he said to the Corinthians, 'not to know anything among you save Jesus Christ and Him crucified' (1 Cor 2:2). Or again: 'For other foundation can no man lay than that is laid, which is Jesus Christ' (1 Cor 3:11). It is always this message of the cross.

And what did they say about it? This is still the heart of the matter. They did not merely announce the fact that he had been crucified on a cross, that he had died and was buried and rose again. No, they expounded what that meant; they unfolded the doctrine concerning it and their teaching is made abundantly plain and clear in the New Testament itself. What they said was this. They said that He had come deliberately into this world in order to die upon that cross. They taught that what was happening there was that God, in the language of the Prophet Isaiah, 'laid upon Him the iniquity of us all' (Is 53:6). They said that God was there dealing with the sins of men and women in the person and in the body of the Lord Jesus Christ. Again let me use the language of the Apostle Paul: 'For he hath made Him to be sin for us, who knew no sin; that we might be made the righteousness of God in Him' (2 Cor 5:21).

That is their doctrine, which they preached and proclaimed everywhere. And the deduction they drew was that this is the only way whereby we can be forgiven, and that was why they put it in the central position. Their preaching was to this effect, that it was specifically the death of Christ that suffices us; that it was not His teaching, or His example. They said, 'If He has not died for us, we remain in our sins, we are unforgiven.' Their contention everywhere is that the death on the cross is God's way of forgiving man and making a way of salvation. We are shut up with that cross and with what it means, so that without believing that He died there for our sins and bore our punishment Himself, there is no forgiveness for us and we are not reconciled to God.

That is the message. And that is the message at which so many have stumbled throughout the ages and at which so many still stumble today. So I want to consider what the New Testament itself has to say by way of a reply to this particular source of offence. 'Blessed is he whosoever shall not be offended in me'—blessed is the man, says Christ, who finds nothing about Me that is offensive to him. Does the cross offend you? Is it a difficulty to you? Is the death of Christ a problem to you, or do you see it as the one thing that matters? Is it the thing in which you glory and rejoice, for which you thank God above everything else? That is the Christian position—that the cross should be to us the gateway into heaven and to a knowledge of God.

Now there are many ways in which men and women find this offensive. Let us sub-divide them into two main categories. There is first of all the indirect way of stumbling at the cross. There are many who stumble at it by never speaking about it at all. They may come to me and say, 'Yes, I believe I want this life you are talking about. I want to get right with God; I see my life has gone wrong; I feel I do not know God and I want to know Him.' And so I ask them, 'Very well, how do you propose to get to know God? What are you going to do about it?' They begin to talk about living a good life, but I ask, 'Where does Christ come in?' 'Oh yes,' they reply, 'Christ is an example to help me.' 'But,' I reply, 'does his death mean anything to you?' And then they hesitate. The death of Christ does not seem to be central, they never mention it. They begin with God, quite apart from the death of Christ upon the cross. There is the indirect stumbling block.

The other way in which people do it indirectly is to talk about the person of Christ and about His life and example. They say, 'Yes, I am tremendously interested in Christ. I find He is, as you say, unique. I think His teaching is incomparable—would that the whole world put it into practice! What a wonderful example He is,' they continue, 'especially to young people. I am considering the imitation of Christ....' They think that that is the way of salvation, following Christ. Again we ask them the question, 'What about His death?' 'Ah,' they say, 'it does not seem to be necessary, I cannot see that it is essential'—they cannot understand that. And so it is that men and women are indirectly offended at the cross and at the death of Christ.

Then there is the direct way—let me put it in detail. There are many people who object directly to this preaching of the cross. They say, 'We like your talk about Christ as the

Son of God; we like your ethical emphasis; we like you to point to His life and its sinlessness and His wonderful communion with God. We like His appeal to young people to forsake all and take up their cross and follow Him, but what is the meaning of this blood? What is this talk about the absolute necessity of His death, and what do you mean by saying we are saved by it? No,' they say, 'we cannot understand that.'

There are two main types of such people and we can perhaps best classify them in the terms that the Apostle Paul uses in 1 Corinthians 1:22–25 — the Greek type and the Jewish type. 'For the Jews require a sign and the Greeks seek after wisdom: But we preach Christ crucified, unto the Jews a stumbling block, and unto the Greeks foolishness; But unto them which are called both Jews and Greeks, Christ the power of God and the wisdom of God.' Notice some of the things that are mentioned by the Greek type. This doctrine of the cross seems to them to be immoral. 'Surely,' someone said to me once, 'we ought to bear our own punishment. If I have sinned, surely I should bear my own punishment. It is hardly fair that another should bear my punishment — it seems immoral. I cannot accept that. I have sinned, I have done the wrong, surely I must bear the consequences myself.' The doctrine of the cross is offensive to a person who speaks like that.

Others say that it is surely wrong to punish one person for another's sins. 'Isn't it,' they say, 'quite immoral that he who was innocent and guiltless should be punished, as you say, for our sin and our guilt?' That is the foolishness to which Paul refers, this idea that it is immoral.

And then someone else puts it in the form of a question. 'I cannot see how one can die for another. What do you mean by this idea? I can understand this person you preach about. I can understand His ethical, moral teaching, but when you say that one has to die for all I cannot grasp it, my mind does not seem capable of receiving it.' This is how the 'Greek' argued and still does.

Then he continues to put it positively, like this: 'Surely,' he says, 'salvation is something that should be the result of man's understanding.' The Greeks always liked philosophy; they believed that what was going to save the world was ideas. They were always looking for new ideas, and there are those who still think that God saves by these ideas. The great need of the world today, they believe, is for one idea to be held before it, and if only someone could put a great idea before mankind the whole world would rise up and put it into practice. Salvation by ideas, by thoughts, by concepts, or by some kind of philosophy. The idea, says the Greek, of one person achieving salvation by dying upon a cross is foolishness.

Then consider the Jewish type. To the Jews the cross was a stumbling block; it was always the greatest source of offence to them, and for this reason. Their idea of the Messiah was that He would be one who would administer great power. He would conquer His enemies and set up a great kingdom. It would be something spectacular and, as a result of that, everyone would recognise Him and, by conquering all their foes, He would deliver and set them at liberty. But here is one who claims to be the Messiah and, in utter weakness apparently, He is crucified upon a cross. 'It is monstrous,' says the Jew. 'The Messiah will be a prince of power. Look at that carpenter of yours, nailed in utter helplessness to a tree—it is imposs- ible. Weakness is the very antithesis of what we expected and anticipated from the true Messiah.'

But there were other things about that cross that offended the Jews; things that still offend all who have the same mentality, and there are many. Jews were offended by the cross because the cross condemned even them. The Jews considered that they were God's people and that all others were Gentiles and outside the fold. But that cross of Calvary means that no one is saved and that everyone is condemned. Though you have the Law and know something about it and have been trying to keep it, while other nations have lived in ignorance, you are as condemned as every other nation; and the Jews disliked that. The cross condemns everybody, for the cross states clearly that people cannot save themselves; the cross is the central proclamation of this fact. The Law was given by God to the Jews, and God said if you keep it, it will save you; but not one of them had kept it.

The cross is, therefore, a standing condemnation of every view and philosophy which says that men and women by their own efforts can reconcile themselves to God, or that they can atone for their sin. To all such views, the answer of the cross is that no one can do this. The cross is the proclamation of the insufficiency of mankind, and people dislike it because of that, for they believe in themselves and in their own power. They believe that they have got it in them to satisfy even the holy God, so when they see that the message of the cross is this condemnation, they are annoyed and offended. They are not annoyed at being told about the person or the teaching, for they fondly think that they could imitate Christ. Even though they cannot keep the Ten Commandments, or the Sermon on the Mount, they fully believe they can imitate Christ and satisfy God. And it is because of such tragic folly and self-confidence that they dislike the doctrine of the cross and find it an offence. So they say, 'Take out your cross and I will believe what your gospel says. Don't talk about "the blood" and I will come to your church.' That is ever a central cause of offence—'Blessed is he whosoever shall not be offended in Me'.

Is this cross a difficulty to you? Is it an offence to you? Are you stumbling somehow or another in the ways I have been indicating; in one, or perhaps all of them together? What is the answer? Well, let me point out that the answer is exactly the same as it was in the last chapter. The first thing we must realise is that our difficulty about the cross, as with the difficulty about the person of Christ, is all due to the fact that we will approach this matter from the standpoint of reason, philosophy and understanding. What we do is this: we talk together, we have our discussions and our debates and we say, 'I cannot see. I cannot understand. It seems immoral to me. How can one bear the sins of another? How can one bear the guilt of another? Is it right? Is it moral? Is it ethical?' And so on we go, round and round in our philosophical arguments and discussions. We cannot see and understand. Of course we cannot! Of course we never will.

The whole trouble, as the Apostle Paul points out to the Corinthians, is just that—that man will persist in facing these great eternal matters theoretically from the philosophical point of view. We have all got a lot of the Greek in us. We are all so ready to sit down and say, 'Let's discuss this wonderful matter', and then spend our lifetime in discussing the doctrine of the cross, not realising we are in a world that is moving and passing and that we may die at any moment. 'How interesting,' we say, and we discuss it and we spend the night arguing about it and we end where we began and we always will.

It was the same in this story about John the Baptist. His followers were arguing and reasoning and trying to understand. But then John did the essential thing, the thing which we must always do if we are ever to get right about these matters. John said, as we have seen, 'Let's go to Him. Let's stop arguing and reasoning and trying to understand him at a distance. Let me send a message. Let me ask the question.' So he did so and got his reply.

And that is my message now. The only thing to do with this message of the cross is to go to Christ again about it, and this is what you find. Let us face the facts. Consider what He did. We are told that He 'set His face steadfastly to go to Jerusalem'. He was warned by His friends not to go there because Herod was waiting to arrest Him; they pleaded with Him not to go, but He set his face steadfastly to go there. He went there deliberately. He knew what was going to happen to Him. Indeed, he prophesied what would happen. He intimated to His own followers that it was about to take place, but He went there deliberately. And you have to explain it. Why did He do that? Well, listen to some of the things that He said. When He prayed to God, He addressed Him as 'Holy Father'. 'Our Father, which art in heaven, *hallowed by Thy name*'—that is His conception of God, not 'dear Father', or 'dear God', but *Holy* Father. That was always His teaching about God.

Then consider the other statement which He made: 'the Son of man came not to be ministered unto, but to minister, and to give his life a ransom for many' (Mt 20:28). Also, when He was on the point of being arrested and Peter pulled out a sword and was going to try to defend Him with it, He told him to put it back. 'Don't you know,' He said in effect, 'that I could easily command twelve legions of angels who would waft me and bear me to heaven without any difficulty. Peter, don't try to defend me—it is unnecessary. I could easily escape death if I wanted to, but I don't want to escape. I have come to fulfil all righteousness so I am not going to ask for angels to come and defend me from a mere handful of men.'

Then just look at Him in the Garden of Gethsemane. The faithful disciples could not stand the strain any longer and had fallen asleep, and there is our blessed Lord in such an agony that He was sweating great drops of blood. And this is what He said: 'Father, if thou be willing, remove this cup from me, nevertheless not my will but thine be done' (Lk 22:42). What does it mean? Oh, it doesn't mean that He was just afraid of death, for if that were so, He would be less than a soldier who dies bravely in war. He would be inferior to the martyrs and confessors. He was not shrinking from physical death. No, instead of arguing and trying to understand the philosophy of the atonement, go to Gethsemane and explain that prayer. 'Father, if it be possible let this cup pass by me—if there is any way whereby I can do the work You have sent me to do without dying, if there is any other way let me take it. But if there is no other way, I will do it.'

That is the meaning of 'the cup'. The death upon the cross was the one thing that He ever asked God if it could be avoided. But it could not. It was an absolute, utter necessity; it was the only way. He must bear our sins, and those sins were going to separate Him for a second, as it were, in eternity, from the face of God and it was the one thing He wanted to avoid. But it was the only way.

Then listen to Him again on the cross as He says, 'It is finished.' What is finished? The work of making a way of salvation; the work that God had given him to do. 'Father,' He says as He expires, 'it is finished. I have done it, the very thing I came to do, it is complete.'

Then after His resurrection, when He appeared to the disciples, He talked to them and explained the whole thing to them. He took them through the Scriptures—read again the twenty-fourth chapter of Luke and you will find it there at length. He said to them, 'Thus it behoved Christ to suffer and to rise from the dead the third day; and that repentance and remission of sins should be preached in His name among all nations, beginning at Jerusalem' (Lk 24:46,47). Now, He said, do you understand it? Do you not see that I had to die and that my dying was the way whereby I made this way of salvation for you?

This, too, is the preaching of the Apostles everywhere. Stop trying to understand; stop talking about 'immoral ideas'; stop bringing in your philosophies and technical language; stop doing that, just face the facts. There He is, listen to what He has been saying. Look at what He has done; how can it be explained? What answer is there? I suggest that there is only one adequate answer, it is the one given by the Apostles when they went around preaching. The message they proclaimed was that God is a holy God, He is light and in him is no darkness at all. God cannot play with sin, and He has told us that. God, they said, revealed Himself to the children of Israel in the Law. He gave them the Ten Commandments and the Law in order to tell mankind that He is holy and that He will punish sin. God has told us that His nature demands it and insists upon it. He has also said that the punishment for sin is death, not only physical death, but especially spiritual death, which means to be separated from Him and cut off from His love for ever and ever—the wages of sin is death.

Now God had revealed that in the Old Testament. All the burnt offerings and the sacrifices of the children of Israel, all the ceremonies of their temple worship, were just a picture of what Christ was going to do and of what He means. The only way whereby we can be saved is that someone perfect should come along and take our sins upon Him and that God should punish them in Him. Then, having done that, God could say with justice, 'I can forgive your sins.' And that is what happened on the cross of Calvary.

'I think it is immoral,' says someone. 'I have sinned, I should therefore bear the punishment of my sin.' But if you bear the punishment of your sin, this is what will happen to you. You will not only die a physical death, you will die eternally, outside God. So if you are going to bear the guilt of your own sin, you are damned, you are hopeless for ever, for God has said that that is the punishment which He will mete out for sin. How foolish it is to talk lightly and loosely that the one who sins should bear the consequences, for if you do so then those are the consequences. No, we are face to face with facts, with something we cannot understand because it transcends human reason. We are face to face with nothing less than eternal life, with this extraordinary paradox that the very God against whom we sin and have offended was crucified himself in the person of his Son and bears the guilt and punishment of sin and thereby tells us that He can forgive us.

That is the message of the cross, so let me put it like this. I do not understand it, I do not comprehend it in its ultimate application, but I view it like this. Here am I in this world of time. I am a sinner, I have sinned against God, not only in actions but in thought. I have forgotten Him, I have been ungrateful to Him, by nature I do not know Him. I have boasted with pride about my understanding and knowledge and pitted my ideas against the teaching of Scripture. Yes, but I have come to see that I can go to my grave like that. Though I spend another year trying to understand these things, I shall understand no more at the end than I did at the beginning. I find that minds much greater than mine have come to the same conclusion. I know I am a sinner, I know I do not know God, I know I am going to die. I want to meet God, I want to be with Him, but how can I do it? I confront this teaching; I see this blessed person; I cannot explain Him in any terms save that He is the Son of God and He tells me that He has come into this world to pay a ransom for my soul. He tells me that He suffered that I might not suffer, that He was dying my death and that God punished my sins in Him. I still do not understand. I listen to the Apostles; they believed the message and their lives were transformed. I see the saints of the centuries, they believed it and became saints. I look at it and I say I don't understand, but, in my failure and in my weakness, I believe it and I will accept it. It is the only way:

> Just as I am, without one plea,
> But that Thy blood was shed for me,
> And that Thou bidst me come to Thee,
> O Lamb of God, I come!

> Charlotte Elliott

So I stop my reasoning and my arguing and I listen to Him, and that is what He says to me. And I, in my helplessness, say, 'Very well, I will trust you. I will put my hands upon your most perfect sacrifice. I yield my life to you'—'the world by wisdom knew not God' but 'it pleased God by the foolishness of preaching to save them that believe' (1 Cor 1:21). Here is a gospel for all, for all have failed and all can be saved by the power of His death and His mighty resurrection. The offence of the cross? In my helplessness I look at it and I do not see its offence, I rather look at it with Isaac Watts who wrote:

> When I survey the wondrous cross
>   On which the Prince of glory died,
> My richest gain I count but loss,
>   And pour contempt on all my pride.

My foolish little pride has done nothing and I pour contempt upon it, for it is then, and then alone, that I find a way to God. Believing in His death for me and my sins upon the cross, I have come to know Him. I know my sins are forgiven and I know that I am a child of God and an heir of heaven. It is by bearing our sins, by dying for us on the cross and by that alone that He saves us. Do you see, do you believe that that is the only way of salvation for you? And have you thanked Him? Are you ready to thank Him now for dying for you? That is the test of a true Christian.

3

The Right Relationship

Now when John had heard in the prison the works of Christ, he sent two of his disciples, And said unto him, Art thou he that should come, or do we look for another? Jesus answered and said unto them, Go and shew John again those things which ye do hear and see: The blind receive their sight, and the lame walk, the lepers are cleansed, and the deaf hear, the dead are raised up, and the poor have the gospel preached to them. And blessed is he, whosoever shall not be offended in Me (MATTHEW 11:2–6).

The claim of the New Testament is that the most practical and relevant and immediate thing in the world today is the gospel of Jesus Christ. It is more practical and more direct, according to its own claim, than any political action that can ever be taken, and it is more immediate in its operation than all the councils and governments and parliaments can ever bring to pass. Here is something which offers us an immediate satisfaction, an immediate deliverance, everything we need. Why, then, is the whole world not running after it? Why is it not at the feet of Christ, looking up into His face, ready to receive His proffered remedy for its ills? And we have seen that here, in these verses, we have what is in reality the answer to that question. 'Blessed is he,' said our

Lord, in his reply to John the Baptist, 'Blessed is he, whosoever shall not find a cause of offence in me.' That is the trouble.

Now we have been considering various things in Him that offend people, the things that stand between men and women believing on Him and surrendering their lives to Him. First there is the problem concerning His person, the amazing doctrine of the person of God. Then the second source of offence is His death. If He is what He claims to be, why did He die on the cross? And in the last chapter we considered this offence of His death in apparent weakness.

Now we come to another stumbling block, another problem that many people have with regard to Him. We can say about this one that it was, perhaps, the peculiar difficulty that was felt by John the Baptist himself. This is the difficulty that often arises in connection with our Lord's activities, in connection with what He does or does not do. Notice the words of our passage; they are very explicit. We are told that when John had heard, in the prison, of the works of Christ, he sent two of his disciples to ask his question. John had been receiving reports of what our Lord was doing—the very things which our Lord tells the messengers to go back and repeat and elaborate again to John: 'the things which we do hear and see'. John had heard reports about these things, these wonderful miracles of healing, and above all the preaching of the gospel to the poor. John had heard all this, even the account of the raising of the dead, and it was as a result of this that he sent his two messengers.

Now, what does all that mean? Well, it seems to me that the only adequate answer to that question is this. John was in trouble, in a little difficulty, about our Lord's activities. John had been saying to himself, 'If this is the Messiah as I thought He was, why does He stop at these works which I hear He is doing? Why doesn't He go on to do other things, if He is the deliverer He is supposed to be?' What were these things? The prophet Isaiah said—and our Lord reacted to his prophecy when he read the Scriptures in the synagogue at his home town in Nazareth (Lk 4:16–21)—that the Messiah, when He came, was to do two main things: He was to do wonderful works of grace; He would work these miracles of healing and He would preach deliverance to the captives. Yes, but it did not stop at that. He would also announce 'the day of vengeance of our God' (Is 61:1,2). Furthermore when he was baptising at Jordan and heard the people murmuring about this, John himself turned upon them and said, I am not the Christ, I am not worthy to undo the latchet of his shoes; 'I indeed baptise you with water, but ... he shall baptise you with the Holy Ghost and with fire'. But then John added the words: 'whose fan is in His hand and He will thoroughly purge His floor and will gather His wheat into His garner but the chaff He will burn with fire unquenchable' (Lk 3:16,17)— grace, certainly, but also judgement. That was John's message of Christ, that was the message of the Old Testament prophet.

Now, John is in the prison, where he hears the reports of what our Lord is doing, the wonderful miracles of healing and the preaching of the gospel to the poor. That is all right, says John in effect, but what about the judgement? Where is the fan that is in His hand? Why doesn't He start thoroughly purging His floor? What is the rest of the message? 'Art thou He that should come', or must we start looking for another? I have no doubt that something like this had been suggested to John by his followers and disciples. They said, 'Master John, if He whom you describe as the coming one, the Messiah, the Lamb of God, is *really* the Messiah, why doesn't He do something about this imprisonment of yours? He can give sight to the blind; He can make the lame walk and cleanse the lepers; He makes the deaf to hear; He can raise the dead. Why cannot He open prison doors and set you free? Is He the Messiah? Is He a true friend of yours? You announced yourself as His herald. You abased yourself. You said that He must have the pre-eminence. You said, "He must increase but I must decrease." Do you think you are right, John? If He really is the Son of God, how can He allow you to suffer and to lie in this prison? If He has the power, why doesn't He use it?'

'Very well,' said John, 'let us ask Him Himself that question.'

Then let us also look at this difficulty as it presented itself, not so much to John and his disciples, but to the Jews in general at that time, for it was the great source of offence to them; and in their case it took this form. Their idea and conception of the Messiah was an almost purely political one. They believed that He would be a great prince, a great power, and that when He came the first thing He would do would be to start a mighty rebellion. He would deliver them from the yoke and bondage of their Roman conquerors, thereby setting them at liberty, and He would announce Himself and set Himself up as King. He would be throned and crowned in Jerusalem; he would reign and they would be supreme.

And here was one who claimed to be the Messiah, the coming one, the one whom they had been expecting. But what did he do? Well, He spent His time in giving sight to the blind, in enabling the lame to walk, in cleansing the lepers and raising the dead and preaching the gospel to the poor people! As the crowd said to Him on one occasion, 'Why don't you declare yourself?' Even his own brothers said to Him, 'If you are the Son of God, come up to Jerusalem and become crowned as King. Start an insurrection, initiate a rebellion, make a great stand against this Roman power, deliver us, set us free. Surely, if you are the Messiah, you will be crowned as King.' Indeed, on another occasion some of them even tried to take Him by force to make him a king. They had just seen him feeding the five thousand. 'Is this the one?' they said. 'It looks like it with this strange, extraordinary power.' So they tried to force Him to become King, but He went up into a mountain himself, alone. That was their stumbling block.

In other words, both John and the Jews were saying to Christ something like this: 'Oh yes, we hear reports about all the wonderful things you have done, but is that all you are going to do? Does that fulfil your ministry? Aren't you going to do anything further? It is all right as far as it goes, but we want something more. Can you produce no other work? Is

that really the final thing?' That is their ultimate question—
that is the offence.

Now, let me put all this in its modern garb, because my
whole ambition and object is to show you that what I have
been putting in that ancient setting is also a very contemporary position. There are those who believe that the Church
should somehow tell the world how to put itself in order. We
are to direct human activities to that end. But the world is still
the same, and this is how it puts its questions today: 'Why
doesn't Christianity put an end to war? If that gospel of yours
is what you claim it to be, if Jesus of Nazareth is indeed the
Son of God, well then, why is our world as it is now?' 'That is
my problem,' says someone, 'You stand there preaching the
gospel Sunday by Sunday, isn't the thing a contradiction in
itself? Men have been preaching that gospel for nearly two
thousand years and yet look at the world. If it is the gospel of
God, why doesn't He do something about the world? When
is He going to introduce a new order; when is He going to
reform society; when is He really going to change the events
of the world and begin to do things for men, something that is
tangible? You stand there and expect conversions; you talk of
sin and of some wonderful experience that men and women
have which is called rebirth, but is that all? When we are
threatened with the possibility of a third world-war and with
nuclear power, are you still just going to preach that personal,
individual gospel?'

Isn't that how it is put today? But it is not only like that.
Here is the second form which the question sometimes takes.
'If that gospel of yours is right and if God is good,' asks
someone, 'then why do so many innocent people have to
suffer in this world? What about the thousands of Christians
who suffered in the Second World War in this country and in
Germany? They did no harm, nor did they desire to do harm
to anybody, yet they have been destroyed. I cannot reconcile
this. If Christ is the Son of God and if your gospel is what it
claims to be, why, oh why, are the innocent allowed to suffer
and the ungodly allowed to succeed and prosper?' The man

who wrote Psalm 73 has put it better than I can. He has given a classic statement of that position.[1] Many are asking that question and that is the thing that prevents them from coming to Christ and believing on him.

Then the third form of the question is this—and how often one hears it—'Yes,' says someone, 'I have heard that message, and in my desperation once when I heard it, I followed the advice I was given, and went to Him direct. I prayed to Him in my sorrow and need; in my terrible trouble I went on my knees and prayed to Him. I asked Him for deliverance, but He did not answer my prayer. He did not seem to hear me—how can I believe on Him? If He is the Messiah, if He so loves me, as you say, that He has died on the cross for me, why doesn't he answer my prayer?' How many thousands have asked that. Parents have asked it about their children who do not seem to be Christians: 'Why doesn't He save them and bring them in?' Husbands have asked it about their wives, wives about their husbands. It is a great source of offence, it is a great cause of stumbling to many. These are the modern phrases of the famous question, 'Art thou He that should come or look we for another?'

So what are we to say to this particular difficulty? First of all let us look at the instruction that is given in these verses with regard to the source of that kind of trouble. Here I suggest to you that, especially in the light of the whole teaching of the New Testament (and indeed of the Old as well, bearing in mind Psalm 73 and various other passages), the trouble arises in this connection for three main reasons.

The first is that we have false ideas and prejudices as to what the Messiah should do when He comes. The trouble with the Jews was that they had certain notions as to what the Messiah ought to do and what He would do. They had prejudices on that subject, and it was because Christ did not do these things that they stumbled at him and finally said,

[1] cf *Faith Tried and Triumphant* D.M. Lloyd-Jones, I.V.P., for a detailed study of this question.

'Away with him' and were responsible for His crucifixion and death. I will not elaborate this but I do want to emphasise that this is always the first cause of trouble. We all start with certain preconceived ideas as to what Christ should do, what the Church should do and what Christianity should do, and because it does not do so we stumble at it and we remain strangers to its wonderful blessing.

The second trouble is this. The whole difficulty in this matter is that we tend to go to Him seeking blessings from Him rather than seeking Him Himself. We only turn to Him in distress. We do not think about Him, we ignore Him, but suddenly we are in trouble and we rush to Christ. But we have only one thing in mind and that is our need. We have desired the gifts rather than the giver. We are concerned about our situation and our problem rather than about our relationship to Him. How easily we can do this! I am not speaking in judgement, every one of us must plead guilty to this. How easy it is to rush into the presence of God when we are in trouble and pray frantically. We don't even stop to ascribe praise and honour and worship to Him, nor do we even stop to think who He is and of His greatness. We are consumed with our own need and position, so we rush in and we make our desperate requests, and because they are not immediately granted, we take umbrage and we say, 'God is not God. If there is a God, if there is a Christ, if He is what He claims to be, why doesn't He answer me?' We have not thought of anything but the blessing we need.

The third difficulty, which we have touched on before, is the whole trouble of trying to understand what is beyond our understanding. It is the initial difficulty of trying to span and encompass the mind of an eternal God with our pigmy little minds. It is an attempt to claim for ourselves an understanding and an insight and a reasoning faculty and logical ability that is big enough to include the eternal and the absolute. It is the initial postulate that I, man, am big enough to understand God completely, and that He can never and should never do anything beyond my understanding and my ability to comprehend. Am I exaggerating? Am I being unfair? Is that not really the background to the case put by the author of Psalm 73? That was his whole trouble: 'Why does God allow this? I do not understand it'; and that is how people still put it. If God is a God of love, why does He allow war? If Christ is Saviour, why does He allow His own people to suffer? And so on.

This question, this querying all means that whether we recognise it or not, we are all born philosophers, and the trouble with philosophers is that they claim that they can understand everything. That is why philosophy, let me emphasise it again, in New Testament terms, is always the greatest enemy of revelation and Christian truth. It wants to know, it claims it is capable of knowing and that is why God has told us through the Apostle Paul that it has 'pleased him through the foolishness of preaching to save them that believe' (1 Cor 1:21), which means that we are put in the faith position; we believe where we cannot understand, we accept the word and the testimony.

There, I suggest, are the three main reasons for this stumbling over what Christ has or has not done. So what, therefore, is the way out of that miserable condition? It is the same answer once more. You see, the only thing to do in a state or condition like that is to imitate the great example set us by John the Baptist. If you are in perplexity, if you are unhappy and uncertain, if you are always arguing with your friends and others—'Why this, why that'—there is only one thing to do. Stop arguing and go straight to Him. Apply immediately at headquarters, come to Christ and bring your questions to Him. Tell him exactly how you feel and ask Him the question, and if you do so, He will give you the answer. He never fails.

How does He deal with this sort of difficulty? Let us again turn to John the Baptist and his friends, and see how our Lord dealt with the question as John put it to Him. You notice that He did not really answer it directly. John asked, 'Art thou He that should come or do we look for another?' In other words, John put the sort of question which we are so fond of putting. He said, 'I have only one question; are you the Messiah or are you not? The answer is yes or no, give me one or the other.' But, you notice, our Lord did not do that, and this is an important point. The whole essence of this matter is that there are certain questions of ours to which the Lord will not give a 'yes' or 'no' answer. What does He do? He does what He did with John. He just sent back to him a repetition of the very things that John already knew. When John had heard in the prison the works of Christ, he sent his question, 'I hear you are doing these things, but when are you going to do other things?' And back comes the answer, 'I am giving sight to the blind, making the lame walk, cleansing the lepers and in addition the gospel is being preached to the poor. John, look at it again, can't you realise what it means?'

Let me put that like this. When you are faced with this kind of perplexity, the first thing to do is always to start with the Lord himself and not with what He is doing. I am not surprised that people ask the questions they do about Christ, because if they are not right about His person, they will never understand His activities, and it is really for this reason that they cannot understand His death. The disciples only understood the meaning of His death after the resurrection; it was when, in the light of the resurrection, they knew that He was the Son of God, that they began to understand the meaning of His death upon the cross. No one will ever understand the doctrine of the cross unless he has grasped the doctrine of the person.

This, in effect, is what our Lord was telling John: 'John, you cannot understand what I am doing. But are you trusting me, do you really know who I am, are you right about me? You see, your question has led you to doubt me in other things. You have allowed the things I am not doing to raise a query in your mind about my person. John, come back to the beginning, be right about me. Now these are the things that I am doing, and you remember how the prophets said that these were the very things I would do when I came. These are the things that have been prophesied of the Messiah. John, don't you see that I am the Messiah, how can I be anything else? Only the Messiah could do these things; here are the works that authenticate Him. As I said to the people the other day, "For the works which the Father gave me to finish, the same works that I do, bear witness of me, that the Father has sent me"' (Jn 5:36).

And that is still the first thing. The works of Christ can never be understood except in the light of His person. So before you try with your philosophy to understand His actions, or lack of them, come back and find Him—who is He? John had come to conclusions about him merely in terms of activities, so consider this story carefully. How can He be explained in any terms save that He is the only begotten Son of God. Start with Him, then, having done that go on to the next step.

The second step is that we must accept His teaching about His work and about what He has come to do. We must not base our opinions on our own ideas or thoughts, we must listen to what Christ has to say. Let us look at it like this. Is there anything anywhere in the New Testament that says that because the Son of God has come into this world, wars will be outlawed and finished? I rather find that it says that even at the end of the times of the age there will be wars and rumours of wars. Then is there any evidence in the Bible to the effect that the coming of Christ and His gospel was going to mean that every generation from that moment was going to be better than the previous one; or that the gospel was going to introduce a great programme of legislation of social reform and betterment and amelioration and mitigation of suffering? Is there anything here that asks us to believe that the gospel's business is to introduce a new world order and to deliver us from our political and international problems and difficulties. Where is it? Has it ever promised to do that? Did it ever claim that that would be the effect of His coming? Did it say that when nearly two thousand years had passed, this world would almost be unrecognisable because of the preaching of the gospel, that it would have so advanced and developed that man would not be able to recognise it as the same world?

No, rather, what it said was that even as in the days before the flood they were eating and drinking and marrying and giving in marriage, until the very day that Noah entered into the Ark, even so shall it be at the end—and it is like that in our own day. Or as it was in the days of Lot: they planted, they sowed, they were giving in marriage until disaster descended upon them, even so shall these things be when the Son of Man comes.

Now, these are the facts that we consider together in our homes. We discuss them, we debate them and we say that if Christianity is what it claims to be, if Jesus of Nazareth really was the Son of God, if His gospel had been preached for nearly two thousand years, then how can the world be as it is? My reply is that He prophesied that it would be like that; He never said that He would put an end to war and trouble. He rather said that while men were still sinners and refused to recognise Him and believe on Him and surrender their lives to Him, there would be wars and rumours of wars, there would be troubles and pestilences and earthquakes and difficulties and disasters. *That* is what He has said. How wrong, how fatally wrong it is to put up our prejudices, our ideas as to what He ought to do, and because He does not do it to say we cannot believe on Him. No, consider what He has said He is going to do and realise that what He has said and prophesied has literally come to pass.

In other words, look at it like this. What He would have us realise is the supremacy and the primacy of the soul. We are all asking questions about the world, about war and about the atomic bomb. We think of Christianity and we argue about the gospel in these terms. Here is the answer Christ is sending back to us one by one today. 'My friends,' says the gospel, 'you are very concerned about the state of society and the world. You are saying, "Why cannot these statesmen do something about the atomic bomb? Why doesn't the Church declare herself?" But the answer of the Church is this: are you as concerned about your own soul as you are about the state of society and about the world? That is your first concern.'

The world is still the world in sin. I cannot predict the future, no one can. I do not know what is going to happen in the world. I agree that we should make every effort we can to avoid war—it is the business of everyone to do that. But the question the gospel sends back is not 'Why are statesmen failing to agree?' but 'Why is there disagreement in your own family life, in your office, in your shop, among you and among your relatives? Why is there discord there?'

How easy it is to be arguing about the international situation and why the gospel does not do this and that. But the gospel is much more personal, it comes back to you. 'John,' said our Lord, 'make sure that you yourself are right, even there in prison, in your relationship to me.' That is the question of the gospel: what about your soul? We have no right to consider these larger questions until we are right about this central one. How can the world be at peace when men and women in the world are like me as I am by nature, proud and jealous and envious. That is true of all of us so it is not surprising that the nations are like that. And how can there be peace among nations until individuals are right, even in their own sphere, to start with. Before you begin to consider great big questions of world order, start with the disorder in your own life and soul. 'John, make certain that you yourself are right.'

Lastly, His message to us is that we must trust Him absolutely and explicitly, even where we cannot understand. That, in effect, is what He was really saying to John. 'I am doing the things you have heard reported of me, it is quite right. Then you say, "Why aren't you doing other things?" But if you really believe that I am the Messiah, the Son of God, cannot you leave it to me? Even about this question of your being in prison and what your friends are saying about my not being concerned about you. John, if you know that I am who I am, cannot you trust me even there in the prison itself?'

That is the final message, and that is the point to which He has been trying to lead us. He wants our utter, absolute, obedience and He wants our implicit allegiance. Faith means that I believe on the Lord Jesus Christ absolutely. Ah, we have all got to learn this lesson—even Paul had to pass this way. He had a thorn in the flesh and he could not understand it. It seemed all wrong to him. He wanted to preach the gospel, but the thorn was a hindrance to him. Three times he besought the Lord to remove it, but this was the answer he got—'My grace is sufficient for thee'. 'I am not taking out the thorn,' said the Lord in effect, 'but I will do something infinitely bigger. I will bless you with the thorn in your side. I assure you that even with the thorn I can do wonders through you.' 'Quite right,' says Paul, 'and I see that when I am weak, then I am strong and I care nothing except that I be right with you.' The place that God would have us come to is the one in which we can say, 'All things work together for good to them that love God' (Rom 8:28)—all things, it doesn't matter what. 'I have learned in whatsoever state I am there with [and thereby] to be content' (Phil 4:11). That is the argument.

I can put it another way. Jesus of Nazareth, the Son of God, confronts us all—especially those who have this particular problem—and this is what He is saying: 'Is it possible, is it conceivable that I who came from the courts of heaven and was made in the likeness of sinful flesh, that I who suffered the contradiction of sinners for thirty-three years and who staggered to Golgotha with the cross on my back; is it possible that I should suffer and be nailed on a tree and bleed and die for you and yet not be concerned about you? Cannot you trust me; don't you believe on me even though you don't understand? Cannot you see that I have done that? There must be some purpose in what I am doing to you now, or even in what I am allowing to happen to you now.' Do not try to understand the mind of God, my friend, for it is absolute and eternal. It was a part of God's wisdom to allow his servant John to be languishing in prison and to be beheaded at the whim of a mere dancing girl. 'But how can you understand the things that happen?' says someone. I do not understand them and I do not attempt to do so but I know that God is love, that His ways are always perfect. I have proved that in the Christ of Calvary. I cannot understand that eternal mind, but I know He orders all things for the good of those who love Him. And there are times when I look forward to being with Him in eternity, beyond the veil, when He will begin to reveal to me and unfold to me the mysteries that baffled me while I was in the world. But in the meantime I take my stand with the great Apostle and say, 'Your grace is sufficient for me; I am content to believe and to trust to you, come what may.'

Get right about Him. Realise that the soul comes first and that it is the relationship of the soul to Him that finally matters. For His promise is that if you are right with Him, whatever this world may or may not do to you, you are right for eternity and you are an heir of the glory of which no one and nothing can ever rob you.

4

The Offence of Christ's Teaching

Now when John had heard in the prison the works of Christ, he sent two of his disciples. And said unto him, Art thou he that should come, or do we look for another? Jesus answered and said unto them, Go and shew John again those things which ye do hear and see: The blind receive their sight, and the lame walk, the lepers are cleansed, and the deaf hear, the dead are raised up and the poor have the gospel preached to them. And blessed is he, whosoever shall not be offended in me (MATTHEW 11:2–6)

The great proclamation of the Bible, as we saw in the last chapter, is that the Lord Jesus Christ, and He alone, is the Messiah of God. He has come into this world and has done His work. He has done everything that mankind needs; in Him is a full and perfect salvation and all who have believed on Him have found satisfaction, complete satisfaction. Here, then, is the mystery which confronts us still in this world—that everything that God has offered us is there available in Jesus Christ. On the other hand here is a world, desperate in its need, which, for various reasons, will not believe on Him, will not accept His message, will not submit itself to Him and thereby receive the blessing which He has to give us so abundantly. That is surely the great problem.

It is not part of our business to compare these things; there are many other urgent problems in the world today and it is no part of the preacher of the gospel to deny that or to say they are not important, because they are. It is important for people that they should be able to live in this world and have food and clothing and shelter; it is vital for all of us to know what our future is to be—whether, for instance, there will be a war or not. These are all extremely significant questions. But as we have seen, the message of this book is that at the back of all those urgent problems, this is the most urgent of all: who is Jesus Christ? Is He the one whom He claims to be? Is He the Son of God, is He the Saviour, is He the deliverer? And is it possible for us really to experience all that He has promised. That is the vital question, and, according to the Bible itself, and especially the New Testament, the central tragedy of the world is that 'He came unto His own and His own received Him not' (Jn 1:11). The rejection of Christ.

The Bible does not hesitate to say that if only every man and woman in the world believed on the Lord Jesus Christ truly, and received from Him the gift He has to give, and practised the life that He indicated, all our other problems would be solved. If only everyone on the earth was a Christian in this New Testament sense, there would be no need to worry about the possibility of war. There would be no more drunkenness, nor would there be any more infidelity and divorce and all the other horrible things that have disgraced the life of mankind in this world of time. If only—!

There, then, is the possibility; there it is confronting us, so why doesn't the whole world believe on Him? We have been considering certain things about Him which offend people: the difficulties concerning His person and His death, and concerning the fact that He does not pronounce judgement or deal with the evils in society such as war and suffering. Now I want to go one step further and consider something else which is still, alas, as it has tended to be throughout the centuries, the cause of offence to many people. Let me put it like this in terms of this passage. It is the offence of our Lord's way of dealing with mankind and with the problems of mankind. It is the misunderstanding that always tends to arise with respect to His teaching concerning His kingdom. As you will find in the pages of the four Gospels, that was a constant source of offence and of stumbling. We see an example of this at the beginning of John 6 where we find our Lord teaching about the nature of His kingdom. Some people who were listening said, 'This is a hard saying: who can hear it?' and from that time, we are told, many of His disciples 'went back and walked no more with Him'. It was because of this teaching about His kingdom or, in other words, His whole approach to mankind and His way of saving.

Now that was part, it seems to me, of the difficulty and misunderstanding that had crept, up to a point, even into the mind of John the Baptist himself. Indeed, our Lord went on to talk about this later when He said, 'Verily I say unto you, among them that are born of women there hath not arisen a greater than John the Baptist: notwithstanding he that is least in the kingdom of heaven is greater than he.' This is partly because 'the very least in the kingdom of heaven' do not stumble at this teaching about the kingdom; they know who Christ is and what He has done on the cross and in His resurrection. They know, therefore, what Christ can do for the individual soul.

But there are many who still stumble at that, even in this modern world of ours: Christ does not seem to be doing what we think He ought to do. We have our ideas as to what Christianity is and our Lord does not seem to be saying the same thing, so we take offence at it, because He does not tally with our preconceived notions and ideas.

We can sub-divide this kind of stumbling quite simply. There were certain things which characterised our Lord's teaching about His kingdom—His teaching about what He has come to do—which always seemed to be a particular source of offence. There was a sort of narrowness about His doctrine which even in the days of His flesh caused people to stumble, and it still does. We have our large ideas about the gospel and what it ought to be doing, and about the kingdom of God, and the real gospel seems to be a much smaller thing and so causes offence.

Let me give you some instances of this. For one thing, our Lord always persisted in talking about the soul and about spiritual things. Take that incident in John 6. Our Lord was speaking about eating his flesh and drinking his blood and the people would materialise it (we always tend to do this), and our Lord had to say to them, 'The words that I speak unto you, they are spirit and they are life.' It is not the flesh, it is the spirit that matters; that was his great emphasis. Our Lord, in other words, never spoke generalities. He did not come—if I may use such an expression—and paint a large canvas. No, he dealt with one particular thing and that was always the soul of man, and the soul of man in its relationship to God.

Now the Jews were very interested in political questions. They always persisted in thinking of themselves as a nation, and the national problem was to them a great issue, so they wanted our Lord, as we saw earlier, to do something about this but He did not seem to do anything of the sort. He talked to a handful of very ordinary common people; He went about in the villages, and seemed to be wasting His time dealing with individual cases of suffering. 'Why,' they thought, 'if this man were truly the Messiah, He would not be bothering like this with individuals, He would be dealing with the great big question and problem. But He is always talking about this soul that is in us, about spiritual matters. Why will He not deal with these other issues?' And that was a great source of offence, as it still is.

Then, so many think of our Lord as just a great teacher. They are prepared, they tell us, to listen to Him as He stands before us as a wonderful moral exemplar. Others think of Him as a great artist who uttered beautiful ideas and thoughts about life, and they classify His teaching with that of the pagan Greek philosophers. But what an utter travesty that is of the New Testament record! No, our Lord always talked about one thing only. He had only one theme and that was the soul of man. He kept on saying that there was something about the individual that was of priceless value. 'What shall it profit a man,' He said, 'if he shall gain the whole world and lose his own soul?' (Mk 8:36). It was as if He looked at His congregation and said to them, 'You are always interested in things, in the world itself; but I am interested in that which is within you which is called the soul; it will avail you nothing, though your whole world is put in order, if your soul is wrong with God.' The soul—that was His constant theme. He persisted in dealing with it and thereby He offended large numbers of people who listened to Him, people who went out, at first interested, but who ended, like the people in John 6, by going home and walking no more with Him.

Now I could give you many examples from the New Testament of our Lord's great and vast knowledge. He always uses it to illustrate this one theme of His, the soul of man and its relationship to God. Only think of many of the illustrations He uses; cannot you see that all of them are just illustrations about the soul? Look at Him in the country standing there with his followers beside an orchard. He seems to be very interested in fruit trees. He talks about them quite often, and seems to know a lot about them. Yet He never lectured on horticulture and the mystery of life in the trees. He could have done so, but He never did, even though people would have liked Him to do that, as indeed they still would. But what our Lord uses is language like this. He says, in effect, 'Do you see the trees of the orchard? They can be either good or bad and you judge the tree eventually by the fruit which it bears. If it bears good fruit, it is a good tree; if it bears evil fruit, it is an evil tree. Now, have you realised that you and your life are remarkably like those trees? For "by their fruits ye shall know them": you have got a soul within you and it is like that tree in the orchard. As man has planted that tree, God has given you a soul and you are going to be judged in eternity by what you have done with your soul. Let him that has ears to hear take heed what he hears.'

He sees exactly the same with the flowers. Our Lord does not only deal with the flowers as flowers, nor with the birds of the air as such; but He again uses them to make the same kind of point. If your Father can clothe the lily of the field, how much more will He clothe you? If God is so concerned about the birds of the air that not a sparrow can fall to the ground without Him, how much greater is His interest in your soul? It is always the same: all His great and vast knowledge used simply to illustrate His great theme of the soul. And, thereby, He offended people. 'Ah,' they said in effect, 'why will he not address us on art or literature or on any one of these wonderful and interesting themes? He is always talking about this soul that is within us and its relationship to God. So it was, and so He continues to speak.

So the vital question for us is not what is going to happen to the world as such, but what is going to happen to me; what of my soul? That is the emphasis and that has generally been a cause of offence to men and women, this narrowness of the gospel, in that it limits its interests to this one question.

But it does not stop at that, because it narrows it down still further; and here was something that annoyed His contemporaries and has continued to annoy people ever since. For our Lord not only talked about the soul, he talked about the *personal*, the individual soul. He also talked immediately and directly to men and women and that is where He stands entirely apart from all the great philosophers that the world has known. Philosophers are interested in the soul as an idea; they are very fond of discussing it and arguing about it as a concept, as a kind of category in their philosophical systems. Our Lord never did that. He was always immediate, always direct. He was always personal in his approach to men and women, and that is something that has offended people right away down the centuries.

This was put, perhaps once and for ever, in a famous phrase uttered by Lord Melbourne who was Prime Minister in Britain in the 1830s. He said on one occasion, 'You know, things have come to a pretty pass if religion is going to become personal.' By nature we are certainly interested in religion. We like to talk about religious ideas and concepts, but the moment the thing is brought right home to us and to our own position, then we say, 'This is impossible, this is becoming personal.' Our thoughts of religion must be general, and yet our Lord was always personal.

There is one classic illustration of this to be found in John 4, where we are given an account of an interview between our Lord and the so-called 'woman of Samaria'. Our Lord was feeling very tired one afternoon, so He sat down by the side of a well while His disciples went to buy bread in the neighbouring town. As He sat there, a woman came along to draw water from the well and they began to talk; indeed they began to have a religious discussion. The woman, being a Samaritan, had got her ideas and views as to where and how one ought to worship. It was all very clever, an able argument, and she was enjoying this religious discussion when our Lord interrupted her. 'Go call thy husband,' He said, 'and come hither'—in the midst of a discussion on religion our Lord became personal, and He always does. If we listen to Him, if we do what John the Baptist did, if we send to Him, if we come to Him, we will find that invariably He puts that particular personal question to us.

So it is not our ideas about God that matter, nor our ideas of what God ought to be doing. How cleverly we can talk about things like that! We say, 'Now if God is a God of love, why does He allow this and that?' And thus we delight in debating about religion. Indeed, there is nothing that is more enjoyable than a religious argument; we can spend hours and days, yes even a lifetime at it. No one ever objects to a religious discussion so long as it never becomes personal, but the moment it does so then that is going too far. But according to our Lord it is *intensely* personal, for the whole question is my relationship to God. Oh, our Lord did not merely talk about God; He did not come merely to talk in general about the soul; He did not come to draw up a number of platitudes about life and about how it can be lived in a world like this.

No, our Lord has come to do something that is directly personal. He speaks to individuals, and addresses people one by one. That is why people cannot understand Him. They say that He ought to be talking generalities, not dealing with ordinary people individually, putting His questions and demanding His answers. But if you read the Book of Acts, you will find that He continued to do that through His servants, the first preachers, the first propagators of the gospel—they were always personal. Consider, for example, what our Lord says in the case of the greatest convert the Christian Church has ever known—Saul of Tarsus. There he goes with his religious ideas to persecute and massacre the Christians, and our Lord appears to him and puts the question to him: 'Saul, Saul'—a personal address—'why persecutest thou me?' (Acts 9:4). That is what matters—'what is your relationship to me'. And that is always the ambition of the gospel. It comes to us with a personal challenge and it demands a personal response.

I do not apologise, therefore, for putting this simple, direct question—the greatest of all questions—what of your soul? Do you know God? Do you know the Lord Jesus Christ as your personal Saviour? I am not asking, what is your idea about Him? I am not simply asking, what do you think of His teaching? I am asking, do you *know* Him? Read this New Testament and you will find that these people knew Him, there is a personal, immediate knowledge. Salvation does something to our individual soul; it changes our whole attitude and position. Christians are people to whom something has happened; it is intensely personal and if we reject that note, it will cause us to be offended at Christ, for Christ is always personal and those who believe on Him thank Him for that above everything else. We thank Him for that because He has not left us with a number of vague, nebulous, religious ideas but has done this personal thing to us.

And then, of course, we must go on to mention one other thing and that is His constant call to repentance. How often this has caused people to be offended and to stumble! It happened during His days on earth, and it has happened ever since. If only Jesus Christ had outlined and given a great programme of life and living and had said, 'That is my idea, follow it,' people would not have been offended at Him. People are not generally offended at Plato or Socrates or Aristotle and the other philosophers. They never annoy people in this way, and the reason for this is that they always tend to flatter us. The philosopher sits down and evolves his theory of life and says, 'That is how you ought to be,' and we say, 'How noble and uplifting,' and we set out to live that kind of life. But our Lord had a strange faculty for annoying people. Some took up stones to throw at Him, and these other people went back and decided to walk no longer with Him. He was crucified on a tree, and the mob shouted out, 'Away with him! crucify him!' What is the matter with Him, what is this cause of offence?

Well, it is partly this preaching of repentance. The effect of our Lord's preaching was to make everybody feel condemned, and nobody likes that. But we must face it; it is an integral part of the preaching of His gospel. Our Lord uses language like this: He said, 'For the Son of man is come to seek and to save that which was lost' (Lk 19:10), and people were furious at Him when He said it because they saw exactly what He meant. When our Lord said that, His implication was that we are all lost and that we need the Son of God to come on earth before we can be saved. By nature we do not like that because we believe that we can save ourselves, so our Lord came and exposed our sin and helplessness to us and His words were: 'Repent, for the kingdom of heaven is at hand' (Mt 4:17). His first word to mankind was to stop arguing and debating, to stop talking about religion, and to face God. 'Thou shalt love the Lord thy God with all thy heart, and with all thy soul and with all thy mind and … thy neighbour as thyself' (Mt 22:37,39). 'Are you doing that?' asks Christ in effect, 'for that is what God demands. What are your thoughts about God? How do you think of Him? What do you say about Him? Face that.' He especially calls us to an acknowledgement of sin, to repentance.

Let me put it like this in contemporary terms. The world today in its state of trouble is very ready to listen to sermons that tell it somehow or another about the application of Christian principles. No one is annoyed at them. 'What wonderful thoughts,' people say, 'what a beautiful conception.' But the message of the gospel is that the world is as it is because you are as you are. You are in trouble and confusion because you are not honouring God; because you are rebelling against Him; because of your self-will, your arrogance and your pride. You are reaping, says the gospel, what you have sown. You have sown the wind and will reap the whirlwind; you have left your God. You have turned your backs on Him. For over a century you have glorified man, culture, education, politics. You have said you can make a perfect world without the Shibboleth of religion. That is why the world is as it is; confess and acknowledge it, for it is the message of repentance. We all dislike that and yet it is always the message of Christ—He called upon men and women to repent, to acknowledge their sin with shame and to turn back to God in Him, but the message of repentance always has been and still is a cause of offence.

Then finally, and perhaps chiefly, what has offended mankind above everything else is the simplicity of our Lord's way of salvation. There is nothing that annoys people so much as the doctrine of the cross, the doctrine of the blood of Christ and of the rebirth. Look at those people whom we read about in John 6. There they are; our Lord has said to them, 'I am the living bread', 'I am the bread of life, I have come down from heaven to give you a new life which is life indeed', and it was that which made them go from Him and decide never to listen to Him again. It was that sort of thing that always infuriated them—when our Lord said He had come to save, they caught up stones and threw them at Him. It is the simplicity of the way of salvation.

Let me put it again like this. If Christ had come and told us that the way of salvation was to consider a great, noble and wonderful teaching and then to resolve to set out and do it, why, we would have liked it. Thoughts of imitating Christ always please mankind, because, as we have seen, they flatter us. They all tell us that if we only use our wills we can do almost anything. So if Christ had come and said in effect, 'I will give you a great example and pattern of how to live, and all you have to do is to rise up and live this life as I am living it,' we would have said, 'Wonderful!' But He did nothing of the kind. Rather, what He actually said was this: 'You are so lost, you are so sinful that you can do nothing about saving yourselves. If any man could save himself,' said Christ in effect, 'I would never have come into this world. God,' he said, 'gave the people in past ages an opportunity of doing this. He gave them a law and told them when He gave it to them, "Do that and it will save you; live that life and you will be righteous in my sight." If man could have saved himself there would have been no need for the Son of God to come on earth.' Indeed, His coming is proof that people cannot save themselves. Our Lord constantly said that and that is what annoyed people so much. He said, 'I have come to give my life a ransom for many, for nothing but that could ever save those souls of yours and reconcile you to God. And,' he said, 'it is as simple as this. I have purchased your salvation, I offer it to you as a free gift.'

But we do not like that; we are all like Naaman the Syrian. He, you remember, had leprosy, so he sent and asked what he could do in order that he might be cured of this disease. And the message was sent back from Elisha saying that he had to go and wash himself seven times in the river Jordan. Naaman was furious, saying that it was an insult. There were rivers at home in his own country which were greater than this rivulet called Jordan, and he was going home in high dudgeon feeling he had been insulted by the prophet of God. But his servants, who were wiser than he was, said to him, 'If the prophet had told you to do some great thing you would have done it, surely you are not going to refuse him when he asks you to do a simple thing. Do what he tells you and you will probably find that the result will follow.' So he did the apparently ridiculous, simple thing and the leprosy was healed.

What a picture that is of the gospel! Is it not the tragedy of all tragedies that what annoys us by nature most of all about the gospel is its glorious simplicity, this statement that we can receive it here here and now, and that we have nothing to do. 'Give me a programme,' says someone. 'Let me write it down in a notebook and I will go out and do it.' No, it is not like that. The message of the gospel is that just as you are, without waiting a moment to rid your soul of one dark spot, just as you are, salvation can be received as a simple gift from the Lord Jesus Christ. Oh that this should have been an offence, that it should still be an offence!

'Do you say,' you ask, 'that I am nobody, nothing? Do you say that I am like someone who has lived in the gutters of life?' I say, my friend, that you are quite as helpless as someone who has lived in the depth of degradation. People cannot save themselves; salvation is the free gift of the grace of God. We must be converted, we must become as little children, we must acknowledge our complete impotence and receive the gift from Him. Do we now understand, I wonder, why our Lord added those words when He sent the message back to John—'blessed is he who shall not be offended in me'? Blessed are those who see Jesus of Nazareth as the Saviour, who see that He has come to deal with us one by one, that He has died for our sins and risen for our justification and that we can receive from Him one by one this wondrous gift of a new life, a new beginning, a new nature, a new outlook. We can become a new creation just by looking to Him and receiving, as little children, His gift divine.

My beloved friend, does He offend you still? Do any of these things about Him offend you? Oh I pray you, see the folly, the tragedy of thus being offended at the Saviour of your soul, your greatest benefactor, and as a little child submit to Him and receive His salvation.

5

Violent People

And from the days of John the Baptist until now the kingdom of heaven suffereth violence, and the violent take it by force (MATTHEW 11:12).

As we look at this twentieth century with all its suffering and bloodshed; as we think about the whole present state of the world in which we live, we must, those of us who think deeply about life, ponder, at some time or another, over the question as to what it is that has gone wrong with the world.[1] What is the matter with man that thus in his folly and in his stupidity he should make such shambles of his world? Why is man so cruel to man, why cannot people live in peace and concord with one another? Why are we unable to enjoy the good fruits of this earth—indeed why must the world be as it is today and as we have known it during this present century. Those are the questions that we must ask ourselves.

They are also the great questions which are posed and answered by the Bible itself. The Bible is a book about life, a book about the world, not something removed from these things. It is not a fairy tale, or a story. Apart from anything

[1] This sermon was preached on Remembrance Day 1948.

else, it is a great book of history; but it is also a book of profound philosophy. It claims especially to treat this very question that is so deeply concerning every responsible man and woman, and it is perfectly clear and specific in its answer.

I am never tired of repeating this, because it seems to me to be the essential message which is needed by the modern world. The whole trouble is due to what the Bible calls sin, our rebellion against God, our disobedience. But, and this is the point, it does not merely stop at diagnosis as do so many of the modern books. It analyses the situation and, after giving the diagnosis, the glory of the Bible is that it offers us a great remedy. We call these four first books of the New Testament 'the Gospels', and 'gospel' means 'good news'. The great good news that the New Testament has to offer is that God has done something, and that if we but believe what He has done and accept this message, we shall be able to be 'more than conquerors' in this present evil world.

That is the position which confronts us, that this person the Lord Jesus Christ, is the Son of God; that the babe who was once lying in a manger at Bethlehem is none other than the second person in the blessed Trinity; that He came from eternity into this world to deal with this very problem that is depressing mankind today—the whole problem of muddle and failure in this world of time. It tells us that He, Jesus of Nazareth, was none other than the Son of God and that He came to earth to do something that has solved the problem of mankind. As we have seen, He offers us a great deliverance, a wonderful salvation, a life of peace and of joy and of satisfaction even in this world; and He holds out to us a vista of glory in eternity surpassing the highest expressions and thoughts of mankind. That is the message of the New Testament—this amazing, wonderful offer.

But if that is true, then why does not the whole world say confidently, 'We are wrong, let us turn back to God, let us believe this gospel of Christ; let us put it into practice and get rid of our problems and live at peace with one another and begin to experience this bliss and joy of which you speak'?

Why doesn't the world believe it? Now that is the theme that is considered here in Matthew 11. We have seen that even while Christ was here on earth, people were in trouble and in difficulty about Him. There were hesitations, queries, things that seemed to confuse mankind and the result was that, though he came into the world to preach and to die, and though the gospel has been preached since by the power of the Holy Spirit, the vast majority of men and women seem to pay no attention to it, ridiculing and dismissing it. Yet there are certain people, as there have been from the beginning, who have believed the message and have gone into the kingdom; they have verified the claims of the gospel and have experienced everything that the New Testament offers.

That is the long story of the Christian Church. There are, in a sense, two histories in this world. The first is the secular history, and then, in addition, there is the other history, that of the Church, the history of God's people, the account of those who seem to stand out and apart from the world; the lives of the saints, the history of ordinary Christian people. So there are two main types of people in the world. There are those who are subject to the world, those who are its victims and who are defeated by it. But then there are those of whom you feel whenever you read an account of their lives that they somehow triumphed. There was something about them that made them different in spite of suffering and adversity and griefs and trials. There remained a happiness, a joy, an exhilaration about their lives which you find in the case of no one else—these were Christian people, God's people. Now that is something which faces us as bare fact in the history of the world, and what I am concerned to do here is to consider with you these people who have believed the gospel and who have gone into the kingdom of God.

Now this is the subject that is dealt with in this verse and I want now, as best I can, to consider this strange and striking and most remarkable statement. What does it mean? As we saw when we looked at verses two to six, John the Baptist sent his two disciples to Christ to ask the question 'Art thou He that should come or do we look for another?' John, temporarily, is uncertain. Our Lord sends back His reply, giving a proof of the fact that He is the Messiah, and then adds the words: 'Blessed is He whosoever shall not be offended in me'.

Then after the messengers had gone back, our Lord turned to the people and began to talk about John. 'What is your view of John the Baptist?' He said to them in effect. 'Don't misunderstand the word I have just sent back to him. Don't think that he is altogether a fool—not at all! John the Baptist is a remarkable man. When you crowded to listen to him in the wilderness, what did you go out to see? Not a man who delivers his message to suit popular taste, but a fiery preacher, a prophet of the Lord. You did not go out to see a man in soft raiment, because those who wear soft raiment are in king's houses and John certainly is not there. He is in prison with chains hanging heavily from his arm. John is not a courtier, nor is he a popular sort of man. He is in prison because he denounced the King's licentiousness to his very face, he condemned the sin. No, do not misunderstand me, John is a prophet, he is the actual herald of the kingdom of God who has gone before me to preach the gospel.'

'And yet,' says our Lord in this verse, 'though John, that amazing preacher, spoke as he did, and though I have been doing these works, the vast majority of you are indifferent, completely unconcerned. You are going on living life as if John had never been and I had never come. Nevertheless, there are certain people who have listened, "from the days of John the Baptist until now the kingdom of heaven suffereth violence and the violent take it by force"; there are some people who have crowded into the kingdom.'

Now that is the general meaning of his statement. But what does he mean by describing the people who have listened and entered into the kingdom as 'violent'? There are those who have believed that this means that the only people who enter the kingdom of God and are converted are those who can be described as violent sinners. Have we not all at one time or another known that feeling? I have had certain people come to me and say, 'You know, I wish sometimes that I had not been brought up in a Christian atmosphere. I wish sometimes that I had been born a pagan and had not attended church or chapel when I was a boy or a girl. I wish I had not been brought up in the realm of these things; I wish that I had been a desperate, violent sinner. I have heard of people in the Salvation Army believing and having a wonderful conversion. They have been terrible sinners, drunkards and wife-beaters and other terrible things, and then they have heard the gospel and believed it and their whole life has been changed. Now I wish sometimes,' say these people, 'that I had been that kind of person, that I could experience this great change that they talk about. Isn't that what is meant by violence?'

Well, clearly, that is an impossible suggestion! If that were true it would mean that God places a premium upon sin. It would mean that God would reward evil and iniquity and violent sin, which is a clear impossibility. God is holy, God is righteous and God can never reward deliberate sinfulness in that sense. But not only do we prove it wrong in that way, we can prove it in another way; for if that kind of exposition were true it would mean that Christian people only belong to that particular type, and that as you examined the long history of the Church you would find that all Christian people belong to a form of that particular pattern. But thank God that is not the case at all! In the Christian Church you will find men and women of every conceivable type. In the kingdom of God are not only men and women who have come right out of the gutter, although, thank God, there are those who have—you can come from the bottomless gutter into the kingdom of God. Yes, but thank God equally that inside the kingdom are men and women who have never been down to the depths in that sense. They have been brought up in a Christian atmosphere and yet they have experienced conversion—I could name many such. Take the classic example of John Wesley and his brother Charles, two men who never committed violent sins, who were brought up in a Christian home and atmosphere and yet were men of whom it could be said that they entered into the kingdom with violence.

No, it does not mean we have to be violent sinners in order to come into the kingdom. What it does mean, I think, is that our Lord's statement could, in effect, be put in this way: 'There are certain people, from the days of John the Baptist until now, who having realised the truth of the message, have been violently anxious to enter into the kingdom of God because they have realised the urgency'. It is another way of describing the sense of urgency.

Let me give you an illustration. Take a man who is in a house that is on fire. The man, by nature, may be quiet and phlegmatic; he may be the sort of person who never seems to get excited about anything at all. But you let that man suddenly find himself in a house that is on fire! Realising that it is ablaze and that if he does not get out very quickly he is going to lose his life, this person suddenly becomes violent and seeks for some fire-escape in order to save his life. He no longer remains phlegmatic; when he realises the position he becomes desperate and urgent, and he begins to move with a strange animation. He is a man who realises the urgency of his position and for the time being becomes violent; he is desperately anxious to make his escape. That is the kind of thing that is indicated in our text here. The only people who enter into the kingdom of heaven, said our Lord, are those who are violent in that sense. The only people who have ever believed this gospel, this great salvation, are those who have realised the urgency of the situation.

Therefore, the question confronting us here is this—have we done so? Can we be described as violent? Have we availed ourselves of the offer of the gospel in this world in which we find ourselves? Our Lord said here, in effect, that what accounts for the fact that so many are outside is that they have never realised the urgency, for if they only did, they would become violent and would frantically seek an entry into the kingdom. But why have they not realised it? That is the question I want to consider now, for it seems to me that this, of all sins, is the particular sin of the generation to which you and I belong.

Now this is not a new thing, of course, because, as I have already reminded you, it is something that has been seen before. Indeed I think I can make out a very good case for saying that it is one of the great major themes of the Bible. Why is it that men and women in this world of time can, as it were, thoughtlessly turn their backs upon this glorious and wonderful message? The Bible says it is because of sin, and what sin does is to drug us; it creates within us a sense of apathy and unconcern. Nothing, according to the Bible, results so much from sin as a kind of paralysis, which is the appalling thing about it. It comes to us as a kind of drug whose effect is to make us sleepy, lethargic and unconcerned. Indeed the Bible from beginning to end is just a great attempt to arouse men and women out of the lethargy and apathy that are the inevitable consequences of sin and evil.

There are endless examples of this in the Bible. Look at them in the Old Testament—was that not the whole trouble with people before the flood? God called a man named Noah and appointed him to preach to the people. 'Flee from the wrath of God' he said. The sin of man has risen up in the sight of God and the very building of that ark was a warning to them; he was urging them to repent of their sin and to become reconciled to God before it was too late. He went on preaching for one hundred and twenty years, and the vast majority of people paid no attention to him. Only eight people entered the ark, and all the others were drowned. What was the reason for this? The answer is the apathy of sin, this drug within it that makes people unconcerned. The same thing was true of Sodom and Gomorrah. Lot remonstrated with those people. He pleaded with them and said, 'God cannot go on allowing this to continue, you are breaking and disregarding His laws, you are violating the sanctities. Terrible judgement must come upon us if you do not listen to Him.' But they dismissed his preaching and his warning.

Indeed, that is the whole story of the Old Testament.

God sent His prophets to the children of Israel with the same message: 'Repent and return to God, for if you do not, God will judge you and enemies will descend upon you. Your city will be destroyed, your temple will be smashed and you yourselves will be carried away captives.' God sent these messengers to plead and to urge them to save themselves before it was too late, but the children of Israel would not listen, and for the same reason—the apathy of sin.

Then our Lord said it was exactly the same while He was here on earth. There was John the Baptist, that amazing prophet of God, the man in the wilderness with the camel-hair shirt, eating locusts and wild honey. He preached Christ, the coming Messiah, but the majority paid no attention. Only a few entered into the kingdom, while the vast majority remained apathetic and dull and utterly unmoved. That is the cause of the trouble.

I think you will agree with me that this is the essence of our modern troubles. Cannot it be shown very easily that this is the particular sin of the twentieth century? Look at the position in this country in the 1930s. In spite of solemn warnings that war was inevitable, that it was coming, how many people believed it? What scorn was poured upon the heads of those who saw it; one man resigning from the Cabinet was told to go home and take a dose of aspirin! That is the besetting sin of this age in which we live: the apathy, the failure to realise the critical position in which we find ourselves, the refusal to realise the urgency of life and of our whole situation. It is still due to sin, but in our day it takes a very special form. It is an apathy about the gospel of Christ which still claims for itself an intellectual basis. Modern men and women have truly persuaded themselves that as the result of their knowledge, this sort of thing really is almost insulting to them. God has been dismissed, people do not think about Him at all. A future life is not even thought of, because we are all living for this present world, the one which we can see.

So the great emphasis of the last hundred years has been upon this life and we have set out to make it as perfect as we can. We have paid more attention to housing, to economics, to money. We want more money so that we can enjoy life; it has all been materialistic. We have disliked anyone who has stood before us and reminded us of the next world; indeed, we are uncertain as to whether there is another world. We have felt that this kind of belief belongs to a vague primitive past. Of course, we expect pagan people to believe in another world beyond death and the grave—but with our scientific knowledge, we have dismissed that. So we have deliberately avoided thoughts of death and thoughts of life beyond death and the grave, we have shut out the spiritual realm and the eternal and the absolute.

Thus modern man in his self-satisfaction has deliberately shut his mind to these things and has concentrated upon living his life in this world, so confident that he can make a perfect world of it. But here we are with our troubles and our perplexities, our wars and alarms and turmoil yet within this fatal apathy, this curious inability to realise the urgency of life, this constant persecution of the prophets, this laughter in the face of all who ask us to bestir ourselves and listen to the message, to do something before it is too late.

Does this not still apply to us? In spite of our world and what is happening in it; in spite of certain portents, the vast majority still say, 'Let us eat, drink and be merry; let us have a good time and enjoy ourselves.' I once read in a newspaper of some film star who said that London was a wonderful place simply because she could eat and drink and be at parties until 3 o'clock in the morning. It is the common attitude throughout the whole of life; most people hold that view: 'Let us live for the moment and make the best we can of life'. It is the apathy produced by sin, the failure to face facts, the refusal to listen to the voice of warning.

Let me put all that in a more positive form. If that is what keeps men and women outside the kingdom, what is it that sends them into the kingdom? 'The kingdom, from the days of John the Baptist until now, suffereth violence and the violent take it by force.' So what is it that makes people 'violent'? Let me put it briefly like this. First of all, it is the preaching of John the Baptist. Secondly, it is the preaching of the Lord Jesus Christ. Now John's manner of preaching was to cry, 'Flee from the wrath to come.' His message was that 'the axe is laid to the root of the trees'; not a mere trimming of the branches; no, more important than that, judgement is announced. He talks about one who is coming, 'whose fan is in his hand and he will thoroughly purge his floor and will gather his wheat into the garner but he will burn the chaff with fire unquenchable'. That was John's message. 'Repent,' he said, 'return to God and realise your sin. Don't you see that all your troubles arise from this wrong relationship to God, so turn back to him.' The preaching of John made some violent, they saw and acted upon it.

What, then, does this mean to us? Let me translate it into simple, modern language. This is the message of the gospel of Jesus Christ to us. First of all there is the preparation through the mouth of John the Baptist. Here we are in this world. We know very little about the actual origin of life, we just find ourselves here. So what is my business here? Is it to live from day to day and to go on living as long as I can, making the best of it, having as much pleasure as I can? Is that all? Surely any man who thinks honestly will see that that is not sufficient; for I see in this life and world not only life but death. Every day I live means that I am a day nearer the end of my life.

Now that is not sob stuff, I am not trying to frighten people; it is facing facts—which is what the gospel always does. The gospel, therefore, both tells me and reminds me of something that I have been trying to forget; that in this world I am a dying man. I cannot avoid it. Of course, I can take my drugs and forget it; I can do everything I can to forget it and the vast majority are doing that. But the gospel says, 'Don't be a fool! Though you may fill your mind with so many pleasures that you may forget the fact of death, every single moment is nearer death, because death is coming.'

And what about that—is death the end? 'No,' says the Bible, 'death is not the end.' We were made by God and in such a way that when we die we do not just cease to exist. It is not like a flower fading and dying, or like the death of an animal. Death leads to a realm beyond, where the Bible teaches we shall stand face to face with God. There is judgement. God our maker is also our judge and everyone of us will have to stand before Him. That was the message of John the Baptist, that is the message of the whole Bible. It is as simple as that, and yet how often do we realise it? How many of us live by that, day by day? How many of us keep on telling ourselves day by day, 'You are dying and you have to face God in judgement beyond death and the grave?'

How, then, will God judge us? He has told us how He will do this. He has told us in the Ten Commandments, in what the prophets preached to the children of Israel, in the Sermon on the Mount, and in the person of Jesus Christ. God has asked us to love Him. He wants us to love Him with all our heart and mind and soul and strength, and our neighbour as ourself—that is the law. A man once asked our Lord, 'What is the law?' Our Lord replied that that is what it demands of us, that is what God wants of us and that will be the test.

'But surely,' says someone, 'isn't all this ridiculous for modern men and women? You should have been here a hundred years ago and said that sort of thing. Don't you know all about modern knowledge and understanding?' But wait, my friend, what knowledge have you which in any way describes what I am saying? Take all the philosophies, take all the science, and all the psychology that have been added to knowledge during the last hundred years. Is there anything in it or about it that can in any way demonstrate to you that what I am just telling you is not the simple, staggering fact? All of us have got to die, and beyond death there stands God in the judgement, and one by one we face him and those are the terms of judgement. And people who realise that, surely, are those who begin to become violent. Yes, they stop talking about the atomic bomb. Rather, they say, 'War or no war, here is something I have to face; this is by far the most important question.' They have realised the urgency.

But let me give you a further proof. Should it not be clearer to us in this generation than it has been for many before us that what I say is the simple truth? Surely the history of this present century really proves the Bible's case. Without God, man cannot live at peace even in this world of time—the wars are a proof of the truth of the Bible. Man without God goes wrong and makes an utter mess of his life and of his world; the very facts of life are proving it. That is the great problem which is confronting the non-Christian philosophers—why is it that the twentieth century, with all its knowledge and learning, seems to be the worst of all the centuries? Why is it that this century, which was meant to be the crowning one of all, should be the one in which men seem to be returning to the dark ages? What is the matter with it? There is only one adequate answer and it is the answer of this old book, the Bible, with its message and call to repentance. Whoever faces that is bound to do something about it, and become violent.

But thank God there is a further inducement to this glorious violence, and it is, as I have said, the preaching of Christ. To see my danger makes me anxious to get at the fire escape; yes, but when I see what He has there waiting and prepared for me, it makes my anxiety infinitely greater. When people see themselves in a lost condition they become alarmed; but when they see the glories of the gospel of Jesus Christ they become still more violently anxious to possess them.

What is it that is offered? Let me give it once more in all its glorious simplicity. The message of Christ, the one who followed John the Baptist, is that He has come into the world to put us right with God. He has died for our sins; He has taken the punishment of them in his own body—that is the meaning of the cross on Calvary's hill.

My friends, your sin can be forgiven, God offers you pardon. Not only that, He offers you a new life, a knowledge of Himself, a life in communion with Himself. He offers to put joy and peace into your heart. Even more than that, He offers you a share in His own glorious life throughout all eternity. He tells you that if you do what He asks you to do and believe on Him, though this world may deal harshly with you, though wars may come and though the world may forsake and kill you and massacre you with other Christians, nothing can separate you from the love of God and there is open for you a great entry into the life of glory beyond death and the grave. That is what the gospel offers and, according to our Lord, it is those who have seen and realised these things who become violent. The vast majority paid no attention, but there were some who were crowding into the kingdom. They were the people who believed what John said, and what Christ said. They saw their danger; they saw the offer of salvation; and they said, 'We must have it; we will not be quiet until we have it.' That is what makes people violent.

Here is the call to repentance; here is the glorious, gracious offer of the gospel of Jesus Christ. I ask again, have we become violent in this sense? 'How can I know whether I am one of those people?' asks someone. And the answer is very simple. There are certain things that always characterise these violent people. To those who realise the truth of these things, this becomes the biggest thing in their lives. These are the days in which we talk about priorities. If you like you can define these Christians, these violent people, in this way: their first priority is this whole question of their relationship to God. They come to see that nothing else matters. Of course they have other interests—these are quite all right. You can go on being interested in your work or your family, it is perfectly right and good. But those who believe the message of John the Baptist say, 'Yes, but before all those other things and of infinitely greater importance is this: where do I myself stand? What if I should suddenly die tonight? I do not know—I cannot afford to take risks about this.' They are like the man who sees himself in danger of being burnt to death and who knows that he must get out, and make certain of this before anything else. Christians are people who make their soul's salvation their first priority. Is that your first priority? Does the question of your soul and your eternal destiny and your relationship to God come before anything else?

The second characteristic of such people is that they are desperately anxious to get into the kingdom of God. Having seen all I have described, they say, 'Nothing matters to me but that I know I am a child of God, that my sins are forgiven, so that whatever may happen, all is right between me and God and I am going to Him.' They seek an entry into the kingdom. Have you done this? Have you really taken up this question? Have you sought for certain to know that you are in the kingdom?

The next thing about violent men and women is that they are very ready and glad to accept the information and the knowledge and the instruction that is given to them. You see, here are people who are in a house that is on fire. They realise that their lives are in danger and the one thing that matters is how they can get at the fire-escape. Then a voice says, 'This is the way.' People who are in that position are not concerned about philosophical insight. They do not say, 'Wait a moment, let's have an argument about this; that was all right for one hundred years ago.' No. Those who realise their danger are very ready to listen to the voice which tells them, 'Follow me, I have come to make a way of escape, come in my direction.'

So men and women who are violent are very ready to give obedience to God. They turn to God and acknowledge their sin. They stop arguing and trying to be clever; they listen to God and what He tells them is that their trouble is moral not intellectual. They are very ready to accept Christ and His wondrous offer of salvation. They do not understand it, but they say, 'Just as I am, without one plea.' Then the same voice tells them, 'Leave your sin and all you are doing which you know to be wrong; turn your back upon the world with its mind and outlook, in all its sin and iniquity, in all its laughter against God, in all its ridicule of the things of the spirit; turn back and follow Christ.' And they are ready to do that. They do not speak of the gospel as being narrow, or say that the

Christian life is restrictive because it prohibits this or that—they do not care what it prohibits if it will set them free. They will give up everything, they will forsake it all. Those who know their problem and hear a voice calling them to a way of escape and salvation do not try to bargain. They say that their soul's salvation is more important than anything else, and at any price they will accept and follow.

The last thing that is true of them is that they allow themselves no rest or peace until they know for certain that they have got it. Come back to my simple illustration. The man in that room knows he will be burnt to death if he cannot get out, and he will try and try and try until he escapes. If you read the lives of the saints, the biographies of God's people, the best people this world has ever known, you will find that that has been true of them—every one. Once they have been awakened to the fact of the soul and the danger of their soul in this world outside the life of God, once they have realised that they have got to meet Him and face Him, they have given themselves no rest until they have found Him, until they have known they are in His kingdom. They have read their Bibles, they have prayed, they have done everything they could. That is always a sign of this violent person.

And what about you? Do you *know* that you are in the kingdom? Do you *know* that you are safe from the wrath of God against sin? Do you *know* God? It sounds childishly simple and ridiculous, but isn't that the trouble with every one of us? Though we know that we are only in this world for a while, that we have got to leave it, and that eternity and God there await us, it is the one question we will not face. We will insure our lives and our health; we will arrange things in order to have a good time, and yet we know it is all temporary, and that it must all come to an end. What is going to be your destiny? What is going to happen to you when you die—you have got to, your soul will go on, it will face God.

Do you not see the urgency of this question? We never know when we will die, but thank God you need not wait a moment. The way of escape is open now; the way of salvation is at hand; you need not wait a second. Just as you are, whatever may have been true of you in the past, you must acknowledge your sin to God and tell Him that you long to know Him and to be right with Him. Tell Him you believe that Christ was His Son and that He came into the world for you and for your sins; that you are going to rely upon that and prove it by forsaking all He demands and by following Christ and living in His strength.

You do that and I assure you you will know your sins forgiven; you will lose the fear of death and the grave; you will know you are in the kingdom of heaven, and you will know what it is to feel that you are a child of God and a joint heir with Jesus Christ. 'From the days of John the Baptist until now, the kingdom of heaven suffereth violence and the violent take it by force.' Press into it, crowd into it! Have you done so? The gate is still open, there is an entry possible here and now.

6

Unbelief

But whereunto shall I liken this generation? It is like unto children sitting in the markets, and calling unto their fellows, And saying, We have piped unto you, and ye have not danced; we have mourned unto you, and ye have not lamented. For John came neither eating nor drinking, and they say, He hath a devil. The Son of man came eating and drinking, and they say, Behold a man gluttonous, and a winebibber, a friend of publicans and sinners. But wisdom is justified of her children (MATTHEW 11:16–19)

I n these verses we return to the same question that we have been considering earlier, why was it that the great majority of the people here in the days of our Lord really seemed to be stumbling at Him and to be rejecting Him? Why was it that, unlike the 'violent' men and women whom we looked at in the last chapter, they failed to see who He was and to accept His gracious offer of salvation? That is the theme which He takes up again here. Now although our Lord put the problem in the days of His flesh, it is a modern question, and quite up to date in the troubled world in which we live, with all the turmoil and unhappiness, the confusion and the discord, and all the consequences of the failure to know God truly. Why is it that mankind will not consider what the gospel has to say—for that is a fact. Those who attend any place of worship are in the minority. The vast majority of people are not concerned; they dismiss, even as His own contemporaries tended to dismiss, our Lord Himself. Why is it that the gospel, which contains within itself the answer to all our questions, and the solution to all our problems, is the one thing that is not being considered? That is the great question.

Our Lord, as we have seen, has already given one great answer. One reason, He says, why men and women do not listen to Him and believe on Him is that they are suffering from the apathetic, lethargic, drugged condition that is always the effect of sin upon mankind. But that is not the only explanation. 'Whereunto shall I liken this generation?' What can I say about it, He asks—there is something apparently so problematical about it—and then He uses a famous picture. He says, it is like children sitting in the market place calling to their fellows and saying, 'We have played the pipes to you and you have not danced; then we have mourned unto you and you have not lamented. What is the matter?'

Now let us understand this picture. Our Lord said that His own generation can be compared to children like that, and it is equally true of all who do not believe the gospel of our Lord Jesus Christ and who have not received its glorious benefits. Children in our Lord's day used to go and play in the great market places, as they tend to do today. When the market had ended there was a big open space and the children went there and this was the sort of game they played. However, there were some children who isolated themselves from the others and who stood looking on. The others had a little conference together and they said, 'Let's start playing pipes and let's invite these other children to join us in our game of dancing and rejoicing.' But the others refused to join them. Then another time they said, 'Let's have a game of funerals. Let's pretend we are mourners; let's put on black clothes or dress ourselves and let's see if they will join us now.' But the majority of these other children would not even do that. And then the first children are peeved, so they say, 'When we ask you to dance with us, you won't do it; when we ask you to play funerals, you don't want to. Whatever we ask you to do, you seem to want the exact opposite.'

'Now,' said our Lord, 'it is like that here. The children of this generation, the people who are outside the kingdom, seem to me to be like that.' 'John came neither eating nor drinking, and they say he hath a devil. The Son of man came eating and drinking, and they say, "Behold a man gluttonous and a winebibber, a friend of publicans and sinners."' In other words, this generation went to John the Baptist and said to him, 'Let's rejoice and be happy,' and John replied to them, 'Repent and flee from the wrath to come.' Then they confronted our Lord and said, 'Now certain things have got to be taken seriously, and there are certain people with whom you should not have anything to do, but you sit down and sup with them—You are the friend of publicans and sinners.

'He seems to be much too cheerful', they say, 'and he is a gluttonous man and a winebibber.' Everything they seemed to want, John or our Lord refused. So here they are in a fit of peevishness and pique, feeling that everything is against them; they refuse to listen and they remain outside the kingdom. Undoubtedly, this is the only way we can explain this picture. Because John came before Christ, no one can say that John came, as it were, piping and asking people to rejoice and dance with him. No, it was the people themselves who wanted to rejoice at that point but John would not, and in the same way, the same people made other demands of Christ and he refused them.

That, then, is our Lord's picture of the outlook and mentality of those who remain outside the kingdom and who refuse His gospel. To understand what it means I suggest to you that we must look at it like this. Our Lord here analyses the state of unbelief, and I think that in the whole realm of Scripture there is no more denunciatory analysis of that state and condition than that which we find here. What is it that keeps people outside the kingdom of God? Apathy? Yes, quite true, but here is something further—it is this terrible condition of unbelief. Let us consider what our Lord has to say about it.

The first thing He tells us is that it is a definite mentality, a definite spirit. Unbelief is not a negative but an active thing. Of course, our tendency is to think of unbelief as just a negative condition in which a man does not believe, but according to the Bible that is an utter fallacy. Unbelief is terribly positive and active, a state and condition of the soul, with a very definite mentality; and the Bible, indeed, does not hesitate to put it like this: 'Unbelief,' it says, 'is one of the manifestations of sin; it is one of the symptoms of that fell and foul disease.' Or, as the Apostle Paul put it in 2 Corinthians 4:4, 'If our gospel be hid, it is hid to them that are lost, in whom the god of this world hath blinded the eyes of them that believe not.'

It is a terrible state and condition. Let me put it like this. It is not just a refusal to believe. That is how the devil foils us, of course—he persuades modern unbelievers into thinking that they are unbelievers because of their great intelligence, their wonderful intellect and understanding. They think that people who are Christians are fools, who have either not read or have not understood what they have read. The unbeliever thinks that he is in that state because of his marvellous brain and mind, and especially because of his scientific knowledge, and that it is in the light of these things that he refuses to believe. 'No,' says our Lord, 'it is not like that. It is much more like those children there in the market place. You notice their spirit; there is a peevishness, an activity about them. You just cannot say they are negative, they are very positive.' That is the whole case which is made by the Bible everywhere.

Unbelievers, of course, do not agree with that, but that is what the Bible tells them. It tells them that they are unbelievers because they are the dupes of Satan, the slaves of sin and of evil. They rejoice in their great emancipation, that they have been delivered from the shackles of the Bible, and that they have been emancipated from this drug, this dope of the people which we call the gospel. Poor things! They are unconscious slaves and, like the victim of many another vice, they do not know that they are victims. It is like a person suffering from some disease without realising it.

They are like that group of children sitting in the market place who talk together saying, 'We are going to decide how the game shall be played and what we will do with ourselves.' They know, they decide when to pipe and when to lament. This is always a characteristic of unbelief. The trouble with all of us in such a state is that we are not prepared to listen and we do not want any information or any instruction. We start with the postulate that we have a theory of life; we know exactly what is needed and therefore we demand it and come to the gospel with our demands. That is the first manifestation of this unteachable attitude. The unbeliever does not come with an open mind, but with preconceived ideas and prejudices, waiting to criticise.

Now let us be perfectly frank and honest with ourselves; we have all known this state and condition. Have we not all tended to approach the gospel, at some time or another in our life, just like that? The most difficult thing in the world is to read the Bible with an open mind. How often people speak of their open minds! 'I am someone with an open mind,' they say, 'it is you Christians who are prejudiced.' My friend, examine yourself again. People with open minds do not dismiss a thing before they have listened to it, nor do they listen with the attitude which says, 'I am going to listen to that but I will reject it.' Open-minded men and women do not decide what their verdict is going to be; rather, they ask, 'Well now, what is this gospel? What has it to say, what has it to give, what are the provisions for life?'

Let me ask a simple question. Can we all say that that is our attitude to the gospel, or are we not by nature like these children? We start by saying, 'We know,' but we have never listened to it. If my attitude towards the Bible is to pick holes in it and not to give it a chance, I am prejudiced, and I am so much in the grip of prejudice that I am determined that the word shall not speak to me. That was the condition of these children sitting in the market place. *They* decided to pipe, *they* decided to lament, nobody else was allowed to say anything, and because the others did not agree, they were annoyed. That, according to Jesus Christ, is always the first manifestation and the tragedy of this state of unbelief. It is unteachable, it is not prepared to listen, it arrives at its decisions and conclusions without facing the facts and examining them in a fair and unprejudiced manner.

Maybe you are not a Christian. You are unhappy, you are facing the problems of life and trying to solve them, and you say, 'What can that old gospel have to say to me?' I ask you, whatever else you may or may not do, I beseech of you, listen to it, give it an opportunity, hear what it has to say. One of the first appeals of the gospel to us all is just to have an open mind and to consider again some of our predetermined conclusions with regard to life and living.

The second manifestation of this state is that it is always changeable and contradictory. I think this follows of necessity, because it is the result of prejudice and not of thought, and also because it is not really based upon true reason but is rather the result of feeling and impulse. So it must be unreasonable and, of course, because of that it is for ever changing its attitude and position, and it is, therefore, very difficult to deal with. Our Lord put that perfectly in the picture. Unbelievers are like those children in the market place; they say, 'Let's pipe and dance,' but the next minute they are saying, 'Let's play funerals, let's mourn.' You never know what they are going to say next. And according to our Lord that is nothing but an accurate description of this state.

Let me put it in modern terms, and in several ways. Take for instance this whole question of the place of intellect in religion, or the place of the intellect in the solution of the problems of life—what are we confronted with? Let me give you facts. You have read, no doubt, about the 'Bloomsbury Set', the intellectuals of the 1920s and 1930s led by people like Mr Aldous Huxley. This group called themselves intellectuals; they said that the great trouble with men and women had been that they had always lived on their feelings. Religion, of course, had been the main offender; it had played on the minds of people. The main need was intellectualism, so the first thing we had to do was to rid ourselves of all that had come from the past, we must be clearly scientifically intellectual. That was the great characteristic of the so-called 'Bloomsbury Set', the bright young people of the twenties, those pure intellectuals who were going to solve the problems of life by rationalism and thought. That is what they told us in the twenties—what are they telling us now?

Well, if you read Mr Aldous Huxley, I think you will find he will tell you that the only hope for the world is mysticism. The trouble with the world, he now tells us, is intellectualism, which is useless. He has tried it and it has led him nowhere. The only hope for the world is for us to be absorbed in the primitive spirit that is behind the universe, there we will find salvation. We must become Buddhists—mysticism is essential because we will never get through by intellectualism. 'We have piped unto you, we now lament unto you.' Unbelief is always changing and contradictory, you never know what it will be telling you next. Follow the developments of the last hundred years in the realm of people who are not Christians and you will find that I am not exaggerating. Our Lord has given a perfectly accurate description of them—all intellect one moment and the next moment it must be mysticism.

Or let me put it like this. Half our time we are being told that this religion of ours is nothing but sob-stuff, all right for women and children, with no intellect, no reason, no thought. But then the constant charge that is being brought by others is, 'that man reasons too much; there is too much argument in his preaching—why doesn't he tell us a story?' Whatever is done seems to be wrong.

Or, to give you another illustration, take the question of good works in religion. You will find the same fickleness and changeableness with respect to this also. When the gospel of Jesus Christ comes to such people it tells them, 'You have nothing to do but to become as a little child. Just accept it as a pauper, take salvation as a free gift. The gospel does not tell you that you suddenly have to do wonderful works. You can do nothing; you are justified by faith.' Yet people feel that this is insulting. 'Fancy telling me,' says someone, 'that I have to become as a little child, it is absolutely offensive to my personality and nature.'

But then if the gospel begins to preach holiness; if it begins to say, 'Strait is the gate and narrow is the way that leadeth unto life;' if it begins to denounce sin in the individual and society, or to talk about the Ten Commandments and the moral law and the Sermon on the Mount and the love of Christ, they say, 'It is impossible; such a gospel is too narrow for people and so it is insulting to them.' Piping and lamenting are always contradictory.

Or take the question of the place of zeal in religion. If we should say that a man cannot be saved by his own zeal, then again we are insulting. But if we call for zeal, we are asked, 'Do you want us to have religious mania?' Or let me put it like this. I once remember a man, a non-religious person, complaining to me about a minister who lived next door to him. He said, 'You know that minister, that colleague of yours, has never spoken to me about my soul. I might as well not have a soul so far as he is concerned.' And then, almost before I had left that man I met another who said, 'That colleague of yours is always talking to me about religion and about my soul.' It does not matter what you do or say, it is always wrong. This state of unbelief is unchangeable, and it is unreasonable.

Let me give you another principle. This mentality, I suggest to you, is one which, as long as it remains, will never be satisfied. That is the most terrible thing of all. It starts with its own demands and it makes its requests, but it is never satisfied and it never finds rest or peace. That is one of the major themes of the Bible. It tells us that the fate of a man who falls into sin is that he is going to be a fugitive and a wanderer on the face of the earth, or, to quote that other sentence, which I am never tired of repeating, 'There is no peace, saith my God, to the wicked' (Is 57:21).

The modern generation criticises the gospel and will not listen to it. It thinks it knows everything, but where is it? Is it happy? Has it found its satisfaction, its peace? The answer is that it does not find peace in this world. Nor does it find intellectual satisfaction—why all the endless changes in the theories and in the suppositions? Why all this futile searching, this clutching at any new idea? Why the popularity of cults and all these other things? No, the world today is obviously in a state in which it does not know. It is unhappy; men and women are asking what the answer to life is, how to find the way of release and escape. No, this generation does not know, and yet it will not listen.

Furthermore, as it cannot find intellectual satisfaction, it cannot find moral satisfaction either. Look at the restlessness in the world, all the pleasure mania. I am not denouncing it; it is nothing but a symptom of the tragedy, the pathetic restlessness of mankind outside Christ. In a sense I do not blame people for doing these things. It is a terrible thing for men and women in a world such as this to spend an evening with themselves. As they look at their husbands and wives and little children, they say to themselves, 'What is the outlook, what is going to happen?' I am not surprised that the cinemas and places like that are crowded, nor that there is this pleasure mania. Men and women are running away, trying to find some satisfaction, and they cannot find it. The world is profoundly unhappy—piping, lamenting—first this, then that, always changing and yet never finding what it wants and needs.

But, according to the Bible, if people die in unbelief they will go on like that to all eternity. Although that is a most alarming and terrible thing to say, according to the Bible, they will spend the whole of eternity looking for the satisfaction they cannot find. Our Lord put it once and for ever in the parable of the rich man and Lazarus, the man who lived sumptuously on earth and ignored the poor beggar at his gate. But now, there he is in hell, and what is he doing? His soul is trying to find satisfaction: 'Send down Lazarus,' he asks, 'that he may quench my thirst' (Mt 16:19–31). As I understand this teaching, that is hell; people eternally trying to find satisfaction and peace and ever failing to do so. It is a terrible, horrible thought and yet there it is, the plain teaching of Scripture. Satisfaction is only to be found in God, and in Christ. Unbelief is a state in which men and women can never be satisfied. They can climb the heights; they can go down to the depths; they can have money and influence; they can have a thousand and one things, but they will never know rest and peace for their minds and hearts as long as they are in a state of unbelief.

Lastly—and this is the supreme tragedy of this position—unbelief is a condition that blinds people to the glorious nature of the truth. It blinds them to their greatest benefits and to their own greatest and highest good. Here they are, like children in the market place calling to their fellows, 'We have piped unto you and ye have not danced, we have mourned unto you and ye have not have not lamented. For,' says our Lord, 'John came neither eating nor drinking, and they say, "He hath a devil." The Son of man came eating and drinking and they say, "Behold a man gluttonous and a wine-bibber, a friend of publicans and sinners." But wisdom is justified of her children.'

What does all that mean. Let me put it briefly like this. The ultimate truth of this unbelief is that it blinded those people to the person of John the Baptist and to the person of the Lord Jesus Christ. There they were, looking at John the Baptist and they said to him, 'Cheer up! why aren't you more cheerful? Here you are eating locusts and wild honey, man, why are you so unhappy?' They wanted him to be happy but he refused, and they said, 'He hath a devil; he is a lunatic. There he is preaching his repentance; he has religious mania.' That is what they said about the last of the great prophets of God, the forerunner of the Lord Jesus Christ and the great messenger of the Almighty and the Eternal. Oh what a horrible thing unbelief is! It makes people call God's appointed servant a fool and a devil-possessed man.

But look at their attitude to Jesus Christ. There He is, a friend of publicans and sinners, sitting down among them and eating with them, and what do they say about him? 'A man gluttonous and a winebibber.' The very Son of God incarnate is among them and see how they speak of him—'this carpenter'. Here is God the Eternal seen walking the earth as a man, working His mighty miracles, having all power in His hands; and they dismiss Him. Unbelief is such an evil thing that it blinds people to the greatest benefactors that the world has ever known.

In the same way it blinds them to the message of these benefactors. John the Baptist preached his doctrine of repentance. When he came to the world, they wanted him to be dancing and piping, but he told them to flee from the wrath to come, and that is the essential part of the message of Jesus Christ. The first thing this gospel has to say is that you are in no position to laugh and jig about. Look at your world; see yourself face to face with God in the judgement. Flee! Repent before it is too late. Do not dance around and feel that you are happy. No, the first thing you must do is to get down on your knees in sackcloth and ashes. You must mourn and lament for your sin; it is an integral part of this message, whether we like it or not.

But thank God it does not stop at that. When men and women have come to see the truth of that and have awakened to the fact of their dangerous position in this world and of that which awaits them, they now feel that they are worthless sinners. They do not know what to do with themselves. They say, 'I have sinned against God, I have forgotten him for so long. I never gave him thanks for all his mercies to me—what right have I to turn to him? Indeed, there is nothing for me but to mourn and lament.' Then as they do so, the Lord Jesus Christ comes and says, 'It is all right.' He does for us what the father of the prodigal son did for him. You remember how the boy went to his father and said, 'Father I have sinned against heaven and before thee and am no more worthy to be called thy son. Make me as one of thy hired servants.' He felt he had no claim upon his father and could not call himself a son. But the father said to his servants, 'Give him a new suit of clothes and put a ring on his finger and kill the fatted calf.' Yes, that is the message of the gospel—it has two sides. John the Baptist and Christ's call to repentance, and an offer of pardon and forgiveness, an offer of such a glorious salvation, because we are heirs of heaven and everlasting bliss.

What a terrible thing unbelief does in blinding the mind to both the messages. People think in their cleverness that they have discovered a contradiction: 'Half your time you are saying, repent; half the time you are saying, rejoice; all most inconsistent.' Not at all! The first thing for every one is to be convicted and convinced of sin. If you have not seen that you are a hopeless and helpless sinner in the sight of God, you have not started being a Christian; for God is holy and absolute and eternal and 'there is none righteous, no not one' (Rom 3:10). The best people the world has ever known have always been most acutely aware of their own sin and their own unworthiness. But once you have seen that, He will breathe peace; He will tell you that you are forgiven, and will call upon you to enter into the joy of the Lord. He will dance with you a holy dance and will feast with you, for He will tell you that you have become a child of God and can receive His life and power, and that beyond death and the grave you are going to be with Him rejoicing throughout the countless ages of eternity.

So we have seen our Lord's analysis of unbelief. May God deliver us from it. May He enable us to see, if we are outside Christ and the kingdom, that we are outside because we are blinded by Satan, held by this foul thing that is standing between us and our greatest benefactor and the most glorious gift a man can ever receive.

7

God's Judgement and the Means of Escape

Then began he to upbraid the cities wherein most of his mighty works were done, because they repented not: Woe unto thee, Chorazin! Woe unto thee, Bethsaida! For if the mighty works, which were done in you, had been done in Tyre and Sidon, they would have repented long ago in sackcloth and ashes. But I say unto you, It shall be more tolerable for Tyre and Sidon at the day of judgment, than for you. And thou, Capernaum, which art exalted unto heaven, shalt be brought down to hell: for if the mighty works, which have been done in thee, had been done in Sodom, it would have remained until this day. But I say unto you, That it shall be more tolerable for the land of Sodom in the day of judgment, than for thee (MATTHEW 11:20–24).

I think you will agree that no more serious or even terrifying words were ever spoken even by our Lord Himself than these words which record His final denouncement of the Pharisees and their rejection of Him. There is something about the very words themselves that cause us to feel a sense of solemnity. The very word 'woe' is most expressive and full of foreboding. It is a sort of alarm, a note that prophesies or predicts the coming of some terrible impending calamity and disaster. We find the same word in the book of Revelation also, and the meaning that it carries there is exactly the same as it is here. There, as we are finally held face to face with certain ultimate pictures with regard to the history of the life of man in this world, we cannot but be filled with a sense almost of terror and of alarm. Yet that is the very word that our Lord used on this occasion, and His references to Tyre and Sidon and to Sodom and Gomorrah have exactly the same effect.

Most people, however ignorant of the Scriptures we may be in this generation, remember something about the story of Sodom and Gomorrah, those cities of the plain that were destroyed by fire and brimstone which came down upon them from heaven. These are terrifying and striking Old Testament pictures of judgement and of disaster, so that the very words used by our Lord Himself here conspire together to give us this impression of something unusually serious and truly alarming.

Now the question is, what made our Lord speak words like these? Well, we are told that He began to upbraid the cities in which most of His mighty works were done because they would not repent; so, in other words, the theme is a continuation of what we have already seen: that of the reaction of men and women to the Lord Jesus Christ, a theme which started with that hesitation on the part of John the Baptist because of his circumstances. In a sense we are here confronted directly with what the New Testament clearly regards as something that was curiously surprising even to our Lord Himself. We are told in more than one place that He 'marvelled at the unbelief' of the people. That is what He does right through this chapter, and we have seen how He has been stating various causes for this unbelief, and showing how it renders us incapable of listening truly to the message of the gospel.

But He does not stop at that. He goes on to this further terrifying reason as to why men and women do not submit to Him. It is that they have never realised the consequences of His coming, the consequences of seeing Him and listening to Him. They have never understood the results that inevitably follow from coming into any sort of contact with Him or any kind of relationship with Him. That is the subject which He deals with here, and He puts it in the form of this announcement of judgement; it is one of His many statements of the doctrine of final judgement. He reaches the point at which He begins to upbraid these cities, in which most of His mighty works were done, because they have not repented. He pronounces judgement upon them and He forewarns them of their state and condition when the final judgement shall come.

This is, of course, another of the great central themes of the Bible. You cannot read it without constantly coming face to face with this doctrine of judgement because it is integral to the whole biblical case. It appears at the very beginning. Even when man and woman were still in a state of ignorance in paradise, God introduced the whole notion of judgement when He gave them one prohibition and warned them of the consequences if they disobeyed at that point. At the moment man fell, judgement was actually manifested and put into practice, and as you go through the whole story you find yourself constantly face to face with this great doctrine. The Bible tells us that history is not something haphazard. It has a beginning and it will have an end. But not only that, there is a kind of responsibility in history and, surely, this is the thing that we so constantly fail to realise; our life in this world is a terribly responsible matter.

Now, clearly, that is not in the mind of the average person today. Look at the carefree attitude of men and women, trying to make themselves happy and comfortable, refusing to think and increasing their pleasures. Whatever else we may say about them, it is certainly true that they have never realised the whole responsibility of life. If the Bible does nothing else, it does that—no one can truly read it without at once gaining the impression that to be in this world and in this life at all is a desperately serious matter because of the whole idea of judgement. If life just ended in death and that was the end of the story, it would not be quite the same. But the whole point of the Bible is to tell us that that is not the case, that our life is derived from God. Furthermore, it tells us that God, having given us the gift of life, having made us in His own image and having put a certain dignity upon us, is going to make certain requests and demands of us. So every one of us is living a responsible life in this world and we shall have to render up an account of our stewardship of that life. It is in the Bible from beginning to end and it is a judgement that not only affects individuals, but groups and nations and peoples as well.

Now I know very well that as we consider a doctrine like this we are going to look at something that the average person of today dislikes very heartily. People have long since protested against this whole doctrine of judgement, calling it harsh, unkind and cruel. They say that they do not like to hear a doctrine like that; life is bad enough without preaching such things. They ask, 'Cannot you tell us something that will help us to get along a bit? Why stand and announce "woe"? With all our troubles in life, is this going to be added on top of it all? No, God is a God of love. We cannot accept these passages in your Scriptures which preach judgement.' They have decided that a God of love cannot possibly say anything like that, and so they say that he has not said it and they take out these passages. But the very facts of life are making people reconsider these pronouncements and they are now beginning to say, after they have extracted all the teaching about judgement, that history is proclaiming it instead.

Their difficulty is that they cannot reconcile words like these with the other things we are told about our Lord Jesus Christ. 'Is that the man,' they say, 'who played with little children, who sat down with publicans and sinners? Is it conceivable that such a person who had such an eye of compassion, who went about healing people and who said, "Come unto me, all ye that are weary and heavy laden;" is it possible that the same person should announce "woe"? Can you reconcile that with the parable of the prodigal son?' And so men and women try their utmost to get rid altogether of this idea of judgement and to say that it is incompatible with their whole conception of God, and of God as a God of love.

I will not answer such objections at length, but I do want to suggest some answers in passing. First, if you take this idea of judgement out of the Bible you have very little left. Whatever we may think or say, whatever may be our opinion, it is here, and it is an essential part of the biblical record. But I would also argue that the idea of judgement, even before we come to this record, is surely essential to any conception of a moral order. Of course, I know that the world does not believe in that—hence the lawlessness of life today and all the muddle which is so evident—but if you believe in moral principles at all, if you believe in law and in government, even as a concept, you must believe in judgement.

Furthermore, even if you do not believe that, you have but to use your eyes. For life teaches us, quite apart from these explicit statements of law and of judgement, that there is a whole idea of judgement in nature. If we break the laws of nature then we will suffer for it. We cannot play fast and loose with such laws. If I do not follow certain rules of health I will suffer. If I put my finger in the fire, I may say, 'I do not believe I will be burnt,' but I will be, and the consequences will follow. This is inherent in nature and in life itself, and so, when you advance to the realm of thought, to believe in moral order at all of necessity carries the idea of judgement with it.

But of course I am well aware of the fact that the real objection to the doctrine of judgement is not so philosophical and intellectual as our friends would have us believe. We all know that children never like the idea of judgement; we have all been young and know it from experience. We always felt when we did wrong that our parents were very cruel when they punished us for it; so the lawbreaker thinks that the whole idea of judgement is somehow harsh. But is such a way of thinking right? Of course it is not! It is the way in which we try to deliver ourselves from condemnation, to justify ourselves to ourselves. I am not facing the fact that I have done wrong; I am facing the one who is rightly punishing me and I am querying whether he is right or wrong in doing so. While I am thinking about him, I am not thinking about myself; it is a very obvious psychological trick and it is characteristic not so much of thought but of childishness.

Or let me put it like this. If there is no principle of judgement in life, it is surely rather unfair to those who try to live a good and decent life. If there is no difference between the good and the bad, is that justice? Is it right that the profligate should reap the same glorious benefits as the man who has suffered and borne the heat and burden of the day in an attempt to live a good life? No, that is an utter lack of justice, it is unfair to the good man. But the trouble is, of course, that we never think of him, we only think of the bad man and we always try to explain the case when we ourselves are the culprits.

But, finally, what demolishes this wrong idea of judgement is this: if God simply pronounced judgement upon human sin without anywhere offering us a way of escape, then there might be something to be said for this feeling that we have within us. But, as our text proves beyond doubt, God never announces judgement until He has first given us a full opportunity. Our Lord Jesus Christ did not walk into Chorazin and into Capernaum and into Bethsaida and pronounce woe upon them on His first visit. Not at all! He did the exact opposite; he manifested love, compassion and mercy. He preached the gospel of salvation to them. He held the door wide open, and it was when they themselves spat in His face that He pronounced woe and judgement. There is no case for objection to judgement. Every opportunity, I say with reverence, that even the love of God Himself could give has been given, and it is only after the cross that judgement is pronounced. We are left without a single plea and without any excuse.

But leaving aside this objection to the very doctrine of judgement, let me briefly unfold to you what our Lord Himself has to say about the principle of judgement and of the way in which the judgement itself will be manifested. There are just three simple principles. First, we shall all be judged in terms of what we have made of the Lord Jesus Christ. Those are the terms of judgement. Our Lord put that very strikingly in this picture. You notice that He compares and contrasts Capernaum, Chorazin and Bethsaida (where He had lived and done most of His mighty works) with Tyre and Sidon and Sodom and Gomorrah. What did he mean by that? Well, if you read the prophecies of Isaiah, Jeremiah and Ezekiel, you will find that there were no two cities that were more frequently denounced by these prophets than the cities of Tyre and Sidon, because of their godlessness, their irreligion, and their antagonism to God, and because of the kind of life they were living. Tyre and Sidon stand out in the prophecies as the last word in that which is reprehensible in the sight of God.

As for Sodom and Gomorrah, they were, as we have seen, given an opportunity—read the story in Genesis 19. But when we consider what the names of these cities suggest to us, then Sodom has become a symbol of everything that is false and ugly in man as the result of the fall. Sodom and Gomorrah suggest a profligacy, born in the very gutters of sin, with marauders walking the streets with eyes that 'stand out in lasciviousness'—those were the characteristics of the life there. Now what our Lord says here on this occasion is that the case of Capernaum and Chorazin and Bethsaida is worse than that of those Old Testament cities.

Now this can mean but one thing, which is that the judgement of all men and women is ultimately going to be in terms of their relationship to the Lord Jesus Christ. Try to find a single word against the moral character of the cities of Capernaum and Chorazin and Bethsaida and you will not be able to. We are not told that the moral life of these cities was the same as that of Sodom and Gomorrah. We can be perfectly certain it was not; there were none of these evil men roaming the streets in their lusts. There was nothing like that at all, and yet they are worse than Sodom and Gomorrah! Why? Here is the answer: *He* had lived in Capernaum; He had walked its streets and made it His headquarters. Not only that, it was there that He had worked some of His most mighty and marvellous deeds. It was out of these cities that people like Peter and Andrew and Philip had come, and where our Lord had manifested His glory in a most signal manner. Yet these people went on living as if He had never come at all; that is the source of judgement.

Let us, then, interpret that in modern terminology. When you and I come to the judgement, there will only be one real question put to us: 'What did you do about the Lord Jesus Christ?' Yet I must go further than that, because the book of Revelation rather puts it like this: when we come beyond death and the grave to stand in that judgement, we shall see the Lord Jesus Christ. 'Every eye shall behold Him', and at once we shall know the question, 'What did we do about Him?' That is what our Lord is saying here. These cities, He says, have had such a marvellous opportunity. What a privilege Capernaum had had! The very Son of God had lived there; He had been among the people and they had seen all this and yet He did not affect their lives in any way. They paid no attention to Him and it is that, He tells them, which is going to be the cause of their condemnation in the judgement.

And that is the position still. We will not be examined at the bar of final judgement in terms of our good works and our morality and our thoughts and our ideas about life. The whole message of the New Testament is to say that Jesus Christ has become a source of judgement. Now this is a very serious, indeed an alarming, thought. What our Lord is virtually saying to these people is this. 'You thought,' He said, 'that you were judging me. You looked at me, you watched me and you expressed your opinions of me. You thought you were the judge. But you are, as it were, the prisoner at the bar. You will come to realise one day that my presence among you was judging you.'

Therefore, what really matters, in one sense, is not what we think and say, but His view of us, and whether we belong to Him or not. It is our reaction to Him that matters. Indeed, the very act of hearing this gospel increases our responsibility, for its whole case is that He has come into the world to do certain things. So has He made any difference to us? That is the first question we have to face. If He had never been in this world, would I be any different? Does He come into my life at all? Is my life in any way affected by the fact of the Lord Jesus Christ? If it is not, then I am in the same position as the people of Capernaum and those of Chorazin and Bethsaida.

Now this is the first and central point in the gospel of Christ, this matter of our relationship to Him. It is not Christian theories and ideas about this, that and the other, though these things follow. There is a Christian view and it is a most important subject, but I must not allow you to be interested in the Christian standpoint on anything until we are certain we are agreed on your view of Christ. The gospel is not a philosophy, but an invitation to a personal encounter, an invitation to have dealings with a person, Jesus Christ, and what matters is my relationship to Him. It is on this that I will be tested at the final bar of judgement. Again, therefore, I ask the simple question: what is Jesus Christ to you? If He could be blotted out of history, what effect would it have upon you? Is He there controlling and moulding your life?—that is the question.

That brings me to my second principle. The way to avoid the condemnation and the judgement, according to our Lord, is to repent—he condemned the cities of the plain because they would not. 'But what does "repent" mean?' asks someone. Let me put it as simply and as directly as I can. Repentance really just means that having looked at Christ, having read about Him, having seen what He was and what He did, I begin to think about life anew and afresh. We all form our own working philosophies in this world, so to repent means that we are no longer content just to go on thinking as we have always done. We stop and ask, 'I wonder if that man was right in what he said? I do not like that preacher, but what about the things he talked about? I do not like his doctrine of judgement, but I wonder if there is something in it after all?'

So the first step of repentance is a readiness to reconsider, to think again. Men and women begin to talk to themselves and say, 'I never thought about that. I have been thinking of my profession and of my family. I have never stopped to think what life is all about. I have never asked, why I have come into it and what is going to happen when I go on—I have avoided it. But now I see we ought to think about it.' And those who do that have started to repent.

But they do not stop at repentance. Now that they have begun to think, they say, 'I have to admit, when I am perfectly honest, that my life really has been lived quite apart from God. I have said, "This is what *I* think, *my* idea is this," and I begin to see that that is wrong, because God did not come in to it at all. I have not gone to the Bible which claims to be the authority and the unique revelation of God. I have made my own god and now I can see that this is wrong.' Men and women who speak like this are following this process of repentance. They are admitting to themselves that they had lived for years without thinking about God, and with no real thought of pleasing Him.

Then, having admitted all that to themselves, they go a step further and see, in the light of all this, that they have no claim on the love of God. They realise that God has made the world and has placed them into it. He has given them privileges, health and strength and loved ones. They have never thought of this, and have gone on in their own way. But now they see that that is a sin against God, and, far from criticising God for judgement, they say, 'I am a sinner and I deserve nothing but judgement. If my own child had behaved like that I should feel it deserved correction, but I have done infinitely worse than that. I have offended against God.' They feel they have no plea, so they get on their knees and acknowledge and confess their sin to God, and tell him that they are not able to come into his holy presence.

That is the next step in repentance, but then they go still further and come to this point. They want to be right with God, they have acknowledged and confessed their sin, and then they come to see that even though they do their best and their utmost they cannot undo the past. They see that all their goodness is never good enough for God. They cry out and

ask, 'What must I do?' And back comes the answer of the
gospel of Jesus Christ, and all that He has done for us. They
hear a voice telling them to submit and to believe on Him, to
surrender their lives to Him, to rise up and go after Him, and
they decide to do so.

Now, repentance includes that. Merely to feel sorry
about your sin is not repentance; that is remorse. Most people
are sorry when they reap the consequences of sins—the
morning after the night before. But that is remorse and not
repentance, because repentance means turning your back
upon what you know to be wrong. It means saying, 'My only
hope is to take up my cross and follow Christ and I am going
to do it, come what may,; and setting out upon that road.
That is repentance and that, according to our Lord, is the only
way to avoid condemnation in the judgement.

If those cities which He upbraided had only repented. If,
instead of trying to justify themselves and to condemn Him,
they had said, 'Master, speak to us. Having seen and wit-
nessed the things you have done, we begin to see who you are,
the Son of God; and we begin to see ourselves wrong.' If only
with Peter they had said, 'Depart from me for I am a sinful
man O Lord.' If they had done that, He would have stretched
out His arm to them and attracted them to Himself and
breathed His message of forgiveness.

But, lastly, anyone who is finally condemned is left without excuse and without plea, because of all that Jesus Christ
makes possible to us. As you think of these cities which are
mentioned in these words, do you not feel the tragedy of it
all? There was the very Son of God among them. They saw
the miracles: the Centurion's servant was healed in Capernaum, so was the nobleman's son. Our Lord lived in a house
in Bethsaida, while Peter and Andrew and Philip came from
there; and it was outside that very place that our Lord healed
the blind man. He did some astounding and amazing things
there and these people knew it all. They saw the change in
those three disciples and in the others; indeed all these things
had been enacted before their very eyes. Now, I ask you, is

there anything to be said for people who can look at all that and then turn away from it with a snarl? What would you say to a man in a burning house who refuses to be delivered by the fireman who, having risked his life by climbing the fire-escape, stands there and offers to take him to safety? What would you say to a man who refused it all? What would you say to the drowning man to whom the life-saving apparatus is thrown, but when all he has to do is to take hold of it, throws it away. That is the position. Jesus of Nazareth—who is none other than the only begotten Son of God—had one great reason for coming into this world. It was because men and women, having sinned, were under the condemnation of the Law and the wrath of God.

You may say you do not like the idea of judgement, but I assure you that it is essentially a part of the gospel message from beginning to end as I have already tried to show you. So I ask you again, are you prepared, in your ignorance, to risk and jeopardise your eternal destiny on a theory or supposition? 'That is fear,' says someone—but is there anything wrong with fear? Is a man who is told he has a growth within him and that if it is not removed it will take his life, is he just being a victim of fear when he agrees for it to be removed? I say he is being a very wise man. Not to be frightened at a warning is not to be sane, but to be foolish. Fear! Yes, it is a good thing. Have you listened to the warning that will save you from disaster? There is an element of fear in the Bible and it is there because of the love of God. He calls us to live the kind of lives He would have us live, but if we do not respond to His gracious call we will perish. He loves the world so much that He brings in this element of fear, but everything we need is provided in Jesus Christ.

Christ came to bear our sins, their punishment and the guilt; everything we need is offered to us there: a new life, a new power, a new hope and everlasting bliss beyond death and the grave—the gospel offers it all. If we pay no attention to it or if we ignore it and dismiss and blaspheme it, what can await us? What remains for us but woe and doom and disaster? May God grant us that, having looked at these cities which our Lord speaks about here, we may see the tragedy and supreme folly of not facing Him and of accepting His offer and of submitting ourselves to Him.

8

Babes

At that time Jesus answered and said, I thank thee, O Father, Lord of heaven and earth, because thou hast hid these things from the wise and prudent, and hast revealed them unto babes. Even so, Father: for so it seemed good in thy sight. All things are delivered unto me of my Father; and no man knoweth the Son, but the Father; neither knoweth any man the Father save the Son, and he to whomsoever the Son will reveal him (MATTHEW 11:25–27).

The theme of this eleventh chapter of Matthew, let me remind you, is to show us our Lord face to face with this question of the way in which men and women seem to be stumbling at Him. He had come into the world, sent by God, to bring to mankind this great salvation, and yet instead of rushing to Him and accepting it and submitting themselves to Him, men and women seem to be in difficulties about Him. We have been considering together the various reasons He gives for this, and now, in these three verses, He has ceased, in a sense, merely to comment. He is making a declaration. He now looks upon this whole situation; and from the failure of man, as it were, He turns to the wonderful thing that God has done. Men and women seem to have failed to appreciate it and to understand it, and yet, says our Lord, that does not detract from its glory; what a wonderful thing it is!

But in doing that, He again divides mankind up, as He has done so often in this section, into two groups; on the one hand there are those whom He describes as the wise and prudent, and on the other those whom He describes as babes. Now according to our Lord, the reason why anyone who is not a Christian is in that condition is ultimately pride, intellectual pride. The 'wise and prudent' are those people who think they know; those people who believe that the wisdom of this world is enough; those people who, living in the world and passing through this pilgrimage which we call time, really feel that they understand it. They think that they are going on with it and that the knowledge and the understanding they have, their worldly wisdom and human philosophy, is really sufficient. And that, says our Lord, is what ultimately keeps men and women outside the kingdom. Now it is important to realise that 'wise and prudent' does not just mean intelligence. Our Lord is not saying that all intelligent people are not Christians; that could easily be disproved by men like Paul and Luke and others, and by some of the great saints of the centuries. No, what He means is this: the wise and prudent are not unintelligent people, but they are people who are content with earthly wisdom and understanding; and our Lord says that men and women who are in that position are not only not in the kingdom, but God hides from them and does not show them the wondrous way of salvation in Christ—'I thank Thee, O Father, Lord of heaven and earth, because thou hast hid these things from the wise and prudent.'[1]

What, then, of the other group, the people who are here described as babes? Now obviously the term does not mean literally physical babes, in the sense of infants, because clearly that would be a contradiction of the history of the New

[1] Unfortunately, the sermon manuscript which deals with this subject at length is missing.

Testament itself and of the subsequent history of the Christian Church. People of all ages know what it is to be converted and to become Christians; there is no specific age for conversion. One can be converted at any point. The gospel does not only convert young people, for the old can be converted as easily as the young, and although psychologists have tried to tell us that this is not so, they are, yet again, flying in the face of facts. 'Babes', therefore, must not be considered in terms of age.

Neither must it be construed as ignorant, or lacking in intelligence or understanding, for again, the very example of Paul and people like that prove that it cannot be interpreted in that way. Whatever else you may think of Paul as a natural man, you cannot describe him as a babe intellectually, because he was one of the greatest intellects of all time. No, the term is used by our Lord as an antithesis to ' wise and prudent'; babes are people who have come to see their own insufficiency. They are those who have the wisdom to see what they do not know; who have used their reason so well that they have seen its limits and have, therefore, to use Paul's phrase, become fools that they may be wise. The babe is someone who says, 'Really, face to face with these things, I am nothing but a babe, I do not know.'

This, of course, is the very opposite to the wise and prudent, who feel that they know a thing or two and, endowed with all wisdom and understanding, really do not need to know more and are therefore impervious to the message of the gospel. The babes, on the other hand, have come to the end of themselves and have realised that they are indeed 'as helpless as babes'. And, with the simplicity of a little child, they are ready to listen, to abandon themselves and thus to receive it. As our Lord put it on another occasion, 'Verily I say unto you, Except ye be converted, and become as little children, ye shall not enter into the kingdom of heaven' (Mt 18:3).

This, then, is the positive way of looking at this whole matter. 'Ah,' says our Lord in effect, 'there are so many people outside the kingdom and outside Christ and it is for that reason. But, thank God, there are many who are going in because they have accepted this way of salvation.' Then what our Lord really does in this verse is to tell us something about this great and glorious way which He himself has come into this world to bring to mankind. 'I thank thee, O Father, Lord of heaven and earth,' He says. He praises God for it, and He openly confesses and acknowledges, to the honour and glory of God, that God's way of salvation is wonderful. 'In spite of those who stumble at it,' He says in effect, 'as I look at those who are going into it, I acknowledge and confess its perfection.'

So the question now must be why our Lord thus praises and thanks God for it, and it seems to me that the answer divides itself up very simply like this. First of all He does so because it is a matter of revelation: 'I thank thee, O Father, Lord of heaven and earth, because thou hast hid these things from the wise and prudent.' Yes, but, 'and *hast* revealed them unto babes—even so Father for so it seemed good in thy sight.' Then He goes on, 'All things are delivered unto me of my Father and no man knoweth the Son but the Father; neither knoweth any man the Father save the Son and he to whomsoever the Son will reveal him.'

What, then, does revelation mean? Let me first put it negatively. It does not mean discovery, or arriving at something as the result of a process of thought. We must not start by thinking of the gospel and its salvation in terms of a quest. Now that has been the popular idea during this present century in particular. People have been interested in discovery. We have all sought after truth, and we have all been on this wonderful quest for reality—ultimate knowledge.

But the New Testament confronts us, as indeed does the whole Bible, with the very opposite of that—revelation. It is not the end of a process where a man, after much reading and studying and meditation and cogitation at last arrives at truth. On the contrary, it is something that God gives to us. It is much more like this. Here we are, as it were, in a building

seeking and searching, trying to find and failing completely;
aware of some great screen, and all we can see is just this
screen and nothing else. We are looking for something, hop-
ing to find it, believing and trusting to our own powers that
we shall eventually arrive at it. Then, at long last, in utter
exhaustion and failure and almost giving up in despair, to our
wonderment and astonishment the screen is suddenly drawn
back and we see an amazing sight. That is the idea. Revelation
is an unfolding, an unveiling, a making clear, something being
shown to us; not our discovery as the result of effort, but
something being put before us and our being filled with a
sense of wonder and amazement.

I suggest to you that without that category, and without
that important key, the Bible is really meaningless to us. What
is the Bible? Well, look at the Old Testament. It could never
be called an account of men and women searching for something; how can anyone honestly say that? No, it is the very
opposite. Isn't this the story: men and women going wrong,
turning their backs upon God, making idols for themselves
and worshipping these gods? But then God goes after them
and speaks to them: God does something and shows them
something—that is revelation, the activity of God. There is
surely no other adequate explanation of the Old Testament
but that. All along it is God coming down and coming to
mankind. Was it not God who called Abraham out of his
country and took him to Canaan and turned him into a
nation? And was it not also God who spoke to Isaac and to
Jacob, that man who was so ready to sin and forget God? God
kept on coming back to him and God gave him a promise.
Then God gave the people of Israel judges and kings; He sent
them prophets, He led them on journeys and He raised up
enemies to take them in order to bring them back to
Himself—it is God all the way through.

But supremely, of course, and this is the great message of
the New Testament, God 'sent forth his Son, made of a
woman, made under the law' (Gal 4:4–5). All along we see the
activity of God, God showing man something. So that is the

starting point; salvation is something that comes altogether from God. And when we put it like that, do we not see very clearly, once more, why it is that so many people reject it? The natural man dislikes the whole idea of revelation. Why? Because he is wise and prudent, so full of his own intellect and understanding. He boasts, 'I am not going to be treated like a child. I find I have it within me and in my own power to arrive at any knowledge that I may desire.' Revelation gives the lie direct to that at the very beginning.

But men and women do not like that, and Paul puts it like this in 1 Corinthians 1:21—he says that it was when 'the world by wisdom knew not God' that 'it pleased God by the foolishness of preaching [the thing preached] to save them that believe'. Here then is the first great principle, and if we are wrong at this point, how can we be right anywhere else? If our starting point is wrong, our whole journey must be wrong. The gospel starts by proclaiming that it is a way of salvation. Its message is not something that man has thought of or achieved, but something that comes out of the mind of God. It is something that God shows and gives; that He has revealed; it is altogether from His side, and man contributes nothing to it.

Having, then, laid that down as an absolute principle, let me go to the second statement. Why is God's way of salvation a matter, thus, of revelation? Why must it be that and not man's discovery and achievement? Well, our Lord partly answers that question for us in this very context; it is the great theme, again, of the whole of the New Testament. Let me put it like this: one of the reasons why it must be revelation and not discovery is the greatness of God. 'I thank thee, O Father, Lord of heaven and earth.' Oh how easy it is to talk cleverly about God and to understand the philosophy of God; to have our religious arguments and discussions. But isn't half our trouble that we forget altogether who God is and what He is? God is the Lord of heaven and of earth! It is inconceivable, almost, our minds are too small to get there. From eternity to eternity, He is the creator, the artificer, the sustainer of everything that is.

We live in a very big world. We do not understand it. It has its scientific advances and knowledge, it is full of discovery. We can go on investigating it for millenia, but we will never unravel the mystery of this world. Then think of the cosmos. Think of the sun and the moon and the stars and all the satellites. Think of all the perfect arrangement of all these forces. Think of the mystery of the atom and all these things. God has brought them all into being out of nothing—'Lord of heaven and of earth'—not only all we see, but also all that we know nothing about and have never even imagined. He is the maker, the creator, the one who rules and who sustains them all, and do we claim that our pigmy minds can span and understand and find a being like that? The greatness of God alone makes it utterly impossible.

But then add to that the character of God. 'I thank thee, O Father'—consider how even our Lord in thus addressing Him adds an adjective. In his high priestly prayer in John 17 He says, 'Holy Father'—no one has ever realised the holiness of God to the extent that our Lord and Saviour Jesus Christ did. Notice, too, how He says in the prayer 'Our Father which art in heaven', 'hallowed be thy name.' Ah, how easy it is to argue about religion: 'I think this, and I don't think that; I don't think God should do this and I believe that.' But do you realise whom you are speaking of? It is God who is absolute light in all His perfection, dwelling in light unapproachable. No man can see God and live and no man has seen God at any time. The greatness and the majesty and the holiness of God.

But look at it from the other side. If the character of God makes revelation essential, how much more does man in his condition make revelation essential. What small creatures we are, after all. Baffled by our own world, we cannot even live decently together. We cannot even manage ourselves, let alone understand ourselves. How often we become annoyed at ourselves! Here we are, small creatures with small minds, unable to tackle problems that are here with us constantly, and yet we would claim that our minds can understand God and find

Him and speak to Him as equal to equal. Read Job 9 and get rid once and for ever of any notion that with your mind, just as you are, you can find God.

But look also at our weakness. Our powers seem to fail us, for even at their very best they are not strong enough and that is why we are so repeatedly and constantly baffled. Then add to it all our sinfulness. We must all frankly face the fact that we are essentially different from God, and as we realise something of His holy nature, we see this eternal contrast. Here is God and here am I, and, after all, what we are concerned with is not a little bit of knowledge about all this, nor some intellectual quest. The thing we are concerned about, says our Lord, is to know God. Listen to Him: 'All things are delivered unto me of my Father; and no man knoweth the Son but the Father; neither knoweth any man the Father save the Son, and he to whomsoever the Son will reveal him.'

Now that surely does not mean knowing about; it means a direct knowledge, an intimacy; it means an intimate acquaintanceship. We are not concerned here about knowing certain of the attributes of God. I do verily believe that by a study of nature men and women should, if they reason plainly and clearly, arrive at a belief in a creator, in a mind behind the universe, as so many of the best modern scientists are now prepared to admit. But we are not concerned merely with knowing certain things about God as creator, or as a power or controller. What we really need is this personal knowledge of God in the sense that when we are in trouble and in distress, we can go to speak to Him and know that He is there. To know that He is hearing us and that we can hear Him and derive blessings from Him; that is what we need, all of us, as we face our failure in life and in this world. When we sin and our conscience condemns us and we are filled with remorse and unhappiness; when the whole world cannot please us and give us rest, then it is that we look and long for God and want something that God alone can give us; that is the knowledge we all need. As the Psalmist puts it, 'As the hart panteth after

the water-brooks, so panteth my soul after thee, O God' (Ps
42:1). He had a desire to know God, and that is what our Lord
is speaking of. What He says here is that 'no man can know
the Father'—you will never know God as Father, He says,
unless I reveal Him to you.

And I think that the reasons are these—the very power
of God and even His holiness and our condition. How can we
know Him? Yet that is our need. Revelation is absolutely
essential; men and women throughout the centuries, from the
very beginning, have been trying to find God and to know
Him. You can see that in many places in the Old Testament.
Look again, too, at the Greek pagan philosophers, that is what
they were after. They sought the meaning and purpose of life,
and there is only one answer. It is that there is a God at the
back of it all and the Greek knew his utter need of Him. We
see this in Acts 17. Paul was visiting Athens and there he
found the place crowded with temples to various gods.
Among them he found one with an inscription 'To the
Unknown God'. That is it. You see, they worshipped Jupiter
and Mars and other gods and yet they felt that there was
another God at the back of them all—this Unknown God.
And men and women have always been trying to find Him.
They want to know Him, believing that there is the final
satisfaction. Yet they cannot find Him, they have never found
Him unaided, because the God whom we are trying to know
as Father is the Lord of heaven and of earth. Revelation is
absolutely essential, and without it we remain in darkness.

But let us also consider the content of the revelation, and
this is surely one of the reasons why our Lord praises God
and magnifies his great name. 'All things are delivered unto
me of my Father'—that is the revelation. Our Lord here just
makes this great claim for Himself once more. He says that
there is no knowledge of God apart from Him, and He means
something like this. He tells us, as He does elsewhere, that
God has really handed over the forces of this world to Him. I
wonder whether we always grasp that as we should? The
creator has handed everything over to His Son, and now it is
all in Jesus Christ.

Therefore, how ridiculous it is for people to talk about arriving at God apart from Him! God has committed everything to Him; Christ is central, Christ is absolutely essential and that is the great affirmation that He makes at this point. On another occasion He put it in these words: 'I am the way, the truth and the life, no man cometh unto the Father but by me' (John 14:6). This, then, is the content of the revelation. He, Jesus of Nazareth, claimed that He was none other than the Son of God who had come to earth, and He said that He had done so because God had sent Him. Men and women had sinned against God and were therefore under His wrath; so God would have to punish their sin, and that would mean death and separation from God. So our Lord came, sent, He said, by God in order to deal with that problem.

So these, He says, are the things which have been 'hid from the wise and prudent and have been revealed unto babes'. Christ is the Son of God and He has come into this world not only to teach and to work miracles. The real purpose of His coming was that He might die on the cross. God sent Him, says the author of the Epistle to the Hebrews, in order to 'taste death for every man' (Heb 2:9). He said He came to bear the sins of mankind in His own precious body on the cross on Calvary's hill. There He was punished for our sins. That is the message, that is the thing that 'the babe' has understood. These things are as simple as that, that God in Christ was making a way of salvation through the cross; that having punished sin there in the person of His only begotten Son, He can now offer free pardon and forgiveness to all who believe in Christ and who believe this fact.

Therefore what have we to do? We have nothing to do but to believe that and to accept it as a free gift. Oh what fools we are! 'Tell me what I have to do,' says someone. 'Work out a programme for me; I am prepared to carry it out if I can find God in that way. I am going to live a good life and make myself a Christian. I will please God.' Out upon the suggestion! That is not God's way. You and I by all our striving and sweating and efforts can never atone for sin. I cannot undo what I have done in my life; I cannot get rid of the blots in the copy book of my existence. They are there and, do what I will, I cannot erase them. Try as I will, I cannot live the life I would like to and I ought to live; all my efforts and striving are useless.

But, thank God, that does not matter, for God's way of salvation is that all my sins and failure and shame have been put upon the Son and dealt with and punished. God forgives me freely, and I have nothing to do except as a little child—as a babe—to believe that and to rest upon it; to say to myself, 'Nothing that I can do can ever put me right with God, and I believe He has done it all. I rest on Him, I believe on Him and I surrender my life to Him. I accept God's gift.'

The wise and prudent by their self-confidence have remained outside the kingdom, but these things have been revealed to babes. The people who go into the kingdom are those who, having realised the utter futility of ever trying to find God themselves or of ever trying to fit themselves to stand in his holy presence, have believed the truth concerning Jesus Christ, that He is the Son of God, that all things are committed to Him and that by dying and rising again He has opened the door of heaven to us—and they rely upon that and that alone. That is the content of the revelation.

So why, then, should we hasten to join the Lord Jesus Christ in thanking God that it is like this? My first reason for doing so is the very fact that there is a revelation at all. When I begin to realise what I, and indeed the whole world, have done against God, the amazing thing to me is that God did not blast the universe out of existence immediately. The extraordinary thing is that God has not turned His back upon me. He could have said, 'I made you perfect and yet you ignore and insult me, so perish in your iniquity.' I could not blame Him if He had said that to me. I have sinned against Him, we have all sinned against Him, and we have no plea that we can offer in His holy presence. So I thank God that instead of turning His back upon me, He has looked towards me and has revealed His way of salvation. I thank God for the fact that I have not been left in darkness and in despair and in the hopelessness of my sin.

But I thank Him also that He has done it in such a way that salvation is possible even for a babe in this sense. I thank God it does not depend upon intellect and understanding, or upon some wonderful achievement of mine. There are so many of us who lack intellect and understanding. We have no time to read philosophy, to grasp the mysteries and to handle these great arguments—but you need not be troubled. When God makes the way of salvation, that is the way that can save a babe. It is a revelation, an unfolding. You may not understand, but you can look at a person, can't you, at the most wonderful person the world has ever seen, Jesus of Nazareth? Look at His portrait in the four Gospels. Have you ever seen anyone like Him, with His compassion and love? Look at the deeds which He performed, and at His life. It is a question of looking, and the one who is a babe intellectually can do so, for that is all you are asked to do: just to look, to believe and to accept the gift that He offers to you freely.

And lastly I thank Him because of what this revelation and salvation bring. 'No man knoweth the Son but the Father, neither knoweth any man the Father save the Son and he to whomsoever the Son will reveal Him.' This is what salvation brings me. It brings me a knowledge of pardon and forgiveness, of reconciliation with God. Yes, but beyond all that, it gives me a knowledge of God. Have you ever considered this text in that way? Have you ever seen the span and the ambit of the gospel of Jesus Christ? Here it is—there is this little babe on the ground in his smallness and weakness and helplessness, yet the gospel gives him a knowledge of the Lord of heaven and earth, the maker, the sustainer of everything that is. What a knowledge! That I, the pigmy creature of time, can know God the infinite, the absolute and the eternal—and know Him as my Father, not as some great, mighty force away in the distant heavens, but as my Father. Those who are interested in Greek words can turn up this word for babes in the original, and you will find that it has a sense of sonship unfolding in it. That is what our Lord was saying: that we, though we have sinned, become in Christ the sons of God, the heirs of heaven and of eternal and everlasting bliss.

What a way of salvation! May I say it with reverence, who but God could have thought of it? Such an astounding way that in our utter nakedness and helplessness He just draws back the veil and reveals it to us perfectly in Jesus Christ. He 'of God is made unto us wisdom and righteousness and sanctification and redemption' (1 Cor 1:30). Everything, all in all, a complete salvation. All you do is to look at the Lord Jesus Christ and believe this record concerning Him. Surrender yourself to Him and accept the gift, and you will know the Lord of heaven and earth as your Father.

9

Knowing God

Neither knoweth any man the Father, save the Son, and he to whomsoever the Son will reveal him (MATTHEW 11:27).

These three verses, 25–27, undoubtedly constitute one of the most important statements which is to be found anywhere in the New Testament itself. If you regard it from the standpoint of sublimity of thought, it is very difficult to think of anything that is superior or greater than this. Certainly, if you regard it from the standpoint of theology and of the vital importance of true doctrinal understanding, there is no statement more pregnant with thought and of greater importance and significance than what we find in these three moving verses. It is indeed a kind of epitomy, or synopsis, of vital and essential New Testament teaching; it certainly holds us face to face with all the great central principles of our Christian faith. And it seems to me that when we think about the birth of Christ and what it means, then we can do nothing better than consider this central statement with regard to the real meaning of everything that we associate with the idea of the advent and the incarnation of the Son of God.[1]

[1] This sermon was preached on 12th December 1948.

Now we saw in our last chapter that there are many outside the kingdom simply because they have not started with the idea of revelation. In other words, the first word of the gospel to us all is that it *is* revelation. It is there; it has been done for you, you need not search for it; salvation has come to you. Is not the whole message of the incarnation, and of Christmas and Advent, that God has done something? So then, the first thing we must do is to listen to what God has said and to what he has done. That is the whole meaning of this category of revelation, and it is because we so often stumble at that initial idea that all our subsequent thoughts with regard to this matter tend to go so hopelessly astray.

So we now move on to consider another of these initial misconceptions, which is the misconception with regard to the whole point and purpose of religion, or specifically of the Christian faith. What are we out for? What are we concerned about? What do we regard as the specific objective with regard to this whole matter? What are we intent upon? Now I want to try to show you in terms of this verse that here, once more, we tend to go wrong at the very start. Our Lord makes this dogmatic pronouncement. He says that no man can know the Father save the Son and he to whomsoever the Son will reveal Him.

So we can look at it like this. What is the purpose of the coming of the Son of God into this world? Why was He ever born as a baby in Bethlehem? What is the meaning of the incarnation? What is the whole point and purpose of His life, His teaching, His death upon the cross and His resurrection? Why did He do it all? The season of Advent of necessity reminds us that we are concerned here with something historical. Certain things have happened in history and here is the claim of this person. So what does He say He has come to do? What is it that He is holding out to us as a possibility? Now those are the questions to which He draws our attention in this unmistakable manner, and I would put the answer like this.

First of all, the ultimate goal and objective is to know

God the Father. That, and nothing less than that, is the goal and objective for which we should be setting out, and it was in connection with this that the Lord Jesus Christ really came. How often, by nature, we think of the whole purpose of His coming in terms which are very far removed from that. Ask the average person why Jesus Christ came into this world and about the essence of His message, and you will get some answers like this. We are told that He came to talk to us about life in general and that He came to teach certain principles as to how life should be lived. If you listen to some people, you would think that our Lord was nothing but some great and exceptional exponent of pacifism, that He came to preach peace in that sense. He was essentially a philosopher and a teacher, they say, with certain views and ideas with regard to life, and He stands out before us as the great and incomparable explanation of those particular views. That was His object and purpose in coming, and that was the portent of His message, the thing about which He was constantly speaking.

Our Lord, therefore, is put into the category of certain philosophers. How often people talk about 'Plato and Socrates and Aristotle and Jesus' and any others in whom they are interested. They say, 'If only the world listened and put these principles into practice, all would be well. The business of the Church is to remind the world of this teaching in order to get men and women to live by them and thereby reform the world.'

Others, perhaps, put it more in terms of teaching which will enable us to live a good life. They say that He has come into the world in order to expose sin; that He was not so much a political and social reformer as a moral reformer, and that He came to teach people how to live and to give them a pattern and example and to exhort them to follow in His steps and live life as He lived it.

Others seem to think that His object in coming was to give us happiness, to give us certain comfortable and comforting sayings and to give us certain experiences. They say that He was a religious genius who had certain experiences Himself, and that if we follow Him, perchance we may ourselves share in those same experiences. He was the greatest religious teacher the world has ever known.

Furthermore, if you ask these people what it means to be a Christian and what the Christian faith really stands for, then this is the reply which you will have. They say that to be a Christian means ... well, that you occasionally attend a place of worship, where you pay your general respects to God and in a general manner acknowledge Him. Of course, you believe that certain things should not be done and that other things should be done. It is a part of the social round, an essential part of our picture of life, something a little bit higher and better than the ordinary run and level of life and living; but that is all, and it stops there.

But here our Lord at the very beginning reminds us that that is not the goal. As Christian people what we should be claiming, and what we should be knowing and experiencing, is not that we have some general ideas or that we are doing certain things and not doing others. Rather, our aim is to know God, to know the Father—nothing less than that and nothing short of it. The Lord Jesus Christ came down from heaven to earth to live and die, and to die in the way He did, to bring us into a knowledge of God. Of course Christians do live a good life; they do have certain general principles and ideas, and they enjoy certain experiences. But that is not their objective. The centre, the ultimate goal of it all is to know God as Father.

But, you notice, our Lord goes on to a second principle which is equally definite and dogmatic. Let me put it like this. This knowledge of God as Father is not, and cannot be, obtained apart from the Lord Jesus Christ. Now this is a very striking statement and obviously it is of the very essence of this matter. You see the boldness of the claim. There stood one in the form of man and 'in the likeness of sinful flesh', speaking as it were as man to man, yet this is what He says: 'No man knoweth the Father save the Son'—'save myself', in other words—'and he to whomsoever the Son will reveal him.' So here, I want to show again, we are face to face with another of those initial misconceptions. Am I exaggerating when I say that this is probably the position in which we have all found ourselves at some time or another? We all start by assuming that our knowledge of God is all right, and if someone tells us that that is the first problem, we feel it is almost being insulting. This is surely the central cause of so many of our subsequent difficulties, namely that we assume we know God, that we assume that this great knowledge is something at which we start. We say, perhaps, we know a certain amount of the teaching of our Lord Jesus Christ. Maybe we have enjoyed certain experiences—'Well, of course, with regard to God, I have always believed in Him; I have always been in the position of a believer.'

But my whole suggestion is that it is just there that we fail—and fail completely. Let me remind you of some of the statements that our Lord made with respect to this important matter. 'No man hath seen God at any time; the only begotten Son which is in the bosom of the Father, he hath declared him' (Jn 1:18)—led Him forth, revealed Him, manifested Him. 'There shall no man,' said God to Moses, 'see me, and live' (Ex 33:20). We think that we know everything about God and that there is no difficulty about our belief in God. My dear friend, ponder a statement like that—you have never seen God! No one can see God and live. God is incomprehensible to man, He is beyond him in His greatness and in His infinity. Consider what our Lord says in John 17:25—'O righteous Father the world hath not known thee; but I have known thee, and these have known that thou has sent me.' There it is once more. He again makes the dogmatic statement that the world as it is, as the result of sin, does not, and has not, known God.

The Apostle Paul puts it like this: 'The world by wisdom knew not God' (1 Cor 1:21)—he is looking back at Plato and Socrates and all that great succession of Greek pagan philosophers. And it is there we see this wisdom of God. God did not send His Son into the world before all those philosophers had appeared. The mightiest thinkers the world has seen and known had already failed to know God before Christ came.

Then take our Lord's famous statement: 'I am the way, the truth and the life: no man cometh unto the Father but by me' (Jn 14:6). Let us look at it like this. Do we not all tend to start by saying, 'Yes, I believe in God, and that He is my Father.' We talk about the 'fatherhood of God and the brotherhood of man'—how much we have heard about these things! 'Yes,' we say, 'God is the Father of every man who is born.' But here are dogmatic pronouncements by the Son of God: 'No man can come unto the Father but by me'; 'O righteous Father, the world hath not known thee'. Indeed, according to the New Testament the central trouble of the world is that it does not know God, and that is the source of all our ills.

For those who may be prone to dispute this dogmatic pronouncement, let me put it to you in this way. What does it mean to know God? Well, very clearly, it does not just mean to know a number of things about God, for we are capable of that. We have seen that a man who uses his reason is someone who ought to be able to deduce that the world must have a creator. I can discover that much about God, but that is not what our Lord means. This term here, 'to know', is one of great intimacy; it is a term which represents a very close kind of knowledge and that is the meaning which it carries here, as indeed it does in all such similar passages. There were people who had 'known' the Lord Jesus Christ; yes, they knew Jesus of Nazareth, but they did not *know the Son*.

No, to know God means that God is not some vague general power behind the world and the universe, but that if I know Him, I know that He is a person. But it does not stop at that. It means knowing Him as a person, not as some great mighty eternal power before whom I cringe; it means that I know Him with a certain degree of intimacy; it means that I know Him as Father. When men and women know God, says the Apostle in writing to the Romans, they address him as 'Abba Father' (Rom 8:15). In other words, when they go on their knees to pray, they do not pray to 'whatever gods may be', nor do they merely offer up a frantic petition to someone they believe may be there. No, they are going to someone whom they know. They go with assurance and confidence to one whom they can thus address as 'Abba Father'. They do not merely know certain things about Him, they realise the presence of God and they know that they are in that presence—it means that.

But it also means that they are aware of God's interest in them and of God's knowledge of them. They also feel that they are known of God as well as that they know God Himself. They are men and women who feel that God is near them, who can say to God quite honestly, in the words of the hymn:

> What if Thy form we cannot see?
> We know and feel that Thou art here.
>
> Henry Twells

They can truly say, 'I need Thee every hour; Stay Thou near by.' They have not seen Him with the eye of flesh but they know, they are aware of the reality of God and of His presence; aware of the fact that God is dealing with them, doing things to them, shaping their lives and speaking to them in His own wondrous way. They are people who know that they are not alone, that in all crises and difficulties in their lives, God is there and the everlasting arms are underneath them. They will never be allowed to fall; they are profoundly conscious that the very hairs of their head are all numbered and that nothing can happen to them without God. That is what is meant by knowing God.

All this is not my theory, nor my imagination, for that is what we are told in the New Testament. Read the teaching of our Lord Himself, read the book of Acts, which contains the experiences of the first Christians. Read the epistles which were written by those men—that is what happened. These people did not believe in some great philosophical 'X'! No, when they pray you feel they are going into the audience chamber; they know there is a person there waiting for them ready to listen to them, one who hears their prayer and who speaks to them. That, too, is what is meant by knowing God.

So, then, let me ask my question once more: Do you know God? Is our Lord exaggerating or merely making a dogmatic pronouncement when He says, 'Neither knoweth any man the Father save the Son and he to whomsoever the Son will reveal him'? Have you by searching found out God? Let me put it still more bluntly; when you pray, have you confidence in your prayer? Is it real or do you just get down and mechanically repeat certain formulae or phrases? Do you have the realisation of the presence of God, for that is what is offered us in the New Testament. That is the priceless thing which the Lord Jesus Christ came into this world to give, to remind us of certain things about God and to introduce us to Him and to make us so to know Him that we can say 'Abba Father' with that degree of intimacy.

I suggest that if we are honest with ourselves, we must agree with what He said. Those who live to themselves can never know God. The best they can do is to pray to the God they hope is there, or to the God of whom they are afraid and whom they partially dislike because of His great power. People, by thought and reason and meditation and good living and everything else, are incapable of knowing this blessed God as their Father.

That, then, brings me to the next principle. Christ came into this world in order to make this possible. So how does he reveal the Father to us? Well, there, I am just asking a question that introduces us to the four Gospels. Go back again to the New Testament and quietly and simply read them with the idea in your mind that we are supposed to know God as Father. Ask yourself, do I know Him like that; have I ever known Him as Father? There in the Gospels you will find that Christ revealed Him in His own life by living a spotless, sinless life. At the end, he turned to His accusers and said, 'Can anybody point a finger at me? Can you convict me of any failure with regard to God or the law?' His life was apart, it was unique, it was perfect; He revealed God by being what He was.

Then He revealed Him in His actions, His miracles—raising people from the dead, healing the sick, giving sight to the blind. Take these things out of the New Testament and what is there left? It is an essential part, it is God in the flesh. It is not difficult to expect miracles if God incarnate is here, and that is what He claims to be. Look at Him in the things He does.

Similarly, He reveals the Father in His teaching. He put it like this: 'He that hath seen me hath seen the Father.' Just before the end, one of the disciples called Philip said to Him, 'Lord show us the Father and it sufficeth us' (Jn 14:8). 'You say you are going to leave us, please don't until you have revealed the Father to us. That is the one thing we want to know. We have had a vague belief in God but we want to know Him as Father.' And then came the reply, 'He that hath seen me hath seen the Father.' In other words, our Lord is saying, 'Look at me, Philip, look at my life and my actions; look at my personality, see me as I am. Look at me and if you do so and see me truly, you have seen the Father.' In everything—in His life, His teaching and His actions, He reveals to us the holiness and the righteousness of God.

Then he taught it by showing God's wrath against sin. 'But what about John 3:16?' asks someone. Listen to John 3:16, my friend! 'God so loved the world, that he gave his only begotten Son, that whosoever believeth in him should not perish'—but apart from Him they would have perished; that is the only way to avoid perishing. Indeed, we also find in John 3 a statement that if a man does not believe, 'the wrath of God abideth upon him' (Jn 3:36). Part of our Lord's teaching about the Father is that the Father is absolutely holy, that He hates sin and has pledged to destroy it and punish it with everlasting destruction. 'Blessed,' He said, 'are the pure in heart for they shall see God' (Mt 5:8)—no one else can see God because only the pure in heart could stand the sight of Him. To look at God is hell to a man unless he has been made pure in heart—'holiness without which no man shall see the Lord' (Heb 12:14). So He revealed the character of the Father as a holy Father.

But He also told us about His love and compassion. That is why, He tells us, He came into the world; it was because of the love of God. He shows us this same love and compassion in His life. That is why He worked His miracles, not simply to heal the people, but to reveal, to manifest His glory and the love and compassion of God. He said, in effect, 'If you do not believe my words, then as I do these things, see the Father in me.' For this holy God is a God of love and compassion. As our Lord went about healing the sick and doing good, so He told us that God is like that. Look again at John 3:16 where he puts it explicitly. And He shows this, too, in the parable of the Prodigal Son where He gives us His teaching concerning the Father's love. He says, 'God the Father is like that, waiting for the Prodigal to come back; not anxious to ostracise him as the other brother was perhaps—no, waiting, seeing him while he was yet a long way off and running to meet him.

'That is God the Father,' says our Lord Jesus Christ—the holiness and the love and the compassion of God.

But surely the most important thing of all is this. How are these things to be reconciled? How can God at one and the same time be holy and yet be compassionate and loving? How can God be righteous and just and view my sin, as He must, according to His own righteousness, and yet have compassion upon me, and pity and mercy, and love me and forgive me? That is the supreme thing that is revealed in the Lord Jesus Christ. He is the revelation, if I may so term it with reverence, of the reconciliation of the holiness and the love of God. For He tells us that the Father sent Him to do and to finish a certain work in this world, which was to do for men and women what they could never do for themselves. He was to render perfect obedience to the law of God and He was to bear the punishment of sin, because the law condemns sin. He came to bear that guilt and punishment, and God, having punished it in Him, can forgive us. So that as I look at the Lord Jesus Christ, I see the holiness and the love of God kissing each other, reconciling each other. Righteousness and peace have met together—but only in Him. There is no way to the Father but by the Lord Jesus Christ.

If I try to get to God without Him I see the holiness only or the love only, but while both are there, I must see both together but I cannot reconcile them. The only place where I see the holiness and the love of God shining out in equal glory and in equal and absolute perfection is on that cross on Calvary's hill. As I look at Him there, I see this Father who said to the woman caught in sin and who was condemned by all, 'Go and sin no more.' I see the one who was absolutely sinless and holy and who nevertheless sat with publicans and sinners. I see this amazing paradox of the two apparently irreconcilable qualities coming together and being perfectly blended. 'No man knoweth the Father save the Son and he to whomsoever the Son will reveal him.' Thank God, in Jesus Christ I am no longer aware of the terror of God. In Christ,

> The terrors of law and of God
>   With me can have nothing to do;
> My Saviour's obedience and blood
>   Hide all my transgressions from view
>
>   Augustus Toplady

In Him I look into the face of God, and lo—it is a Father's face.

10

All Things...

*All things are delivered unto me of my Father, and no man
knoweth the Son, but the Father* (MATTHEW 11:27).

We saw in the previous chapter how our Lord does
not hesitate to make the dogmatic pronouncement
that it is only as He reveals the Father to us that any
one of us can ever know Him: 'neither knoweth any man the
Father save the Son and he to whomsoever the Son will reveal
him.' Now we go on to look at the first part of verse 27:[1] to
consider together this person who is the very centre of the
New Testament and of its history and teaching. The great
questions are, who is He; what is the meaning of Christmas
Day; what is it exactly that we celebrate? As we think of the
coming to earth of one called Jesus of Nazareth, why should
we do so? Is this a kind of anachronism in the modern world?
Are we in our folly celebrating some ancient custom, very
beautiful in its way, a kind of folk lore or story coming down
from the past? Is our belief and interest in these things com-
parable to that of children in Santa Claus? Is this something
that is a reality or is it not? Those are the questions, it seems to
me, that we ought to be facing at a time like this. What is it all

[1] This sermon was preached on 19th December 1948.

about, what is its meaning, what is its purpose? Is it all irrelevant to this life and world and the state in which we find ourselves in society today?

Well, I think the answer to all that depends upon this— who is He? That is *the* question. The significance of Jesus of Nazareth entirely depends upon who this person is. We shall never know exactly what He stood for, nor why He came into this world unless we know who He is, and so I make no apology for putting my question in a simple, direct and personal manner. What is Jesus of Nazareth to us; what do we make of this Christmas business? When we sit down and really think about it– I take it we have done so, or are we in the position that we have never faced it at all? It just comes year after year and we feel it is beautiful and we know about it all—but if we have done this, we have asked ourselves, 'What does this really mean to me, what does it represent? Why am I at all interested, why do I go to a place of worship; why, by so doing, do I put myself into a different category from the vast majority of people who, at Christmas time, are simply thinking of some festivities in which they are going to indulge? What is this Christ, this Jesus of Nazareth, to me? Who is He and what is the truth about Him? If He is the Son of God, why did He ever come into this world?'

Now I suggest that there are no more urgent questions that we can ever face than those, and I want to show you that on these questions depends what I do not hesitate to describe as the most important fact in connection with our life in this world. It is by facing such questions that men and women in the past have come to a real knowledge of Him. That is the key to Christian experience; to face the fact of Jesus Christ and to know who He is; for any experience we may have apart from that is ultimately of no lasting value to us.

Here, then, I want to show how our Lord deals with the question of His own person in a very plain and explicit manner, and in doing so, shows us the whole point and purpose of His coming into this world. So we shall concentrate our attention on this by putting it in the form of the following principles.

Let us start with the astounding claim which He makes for Himself. I use my words advisedly; it is an amazing, incredible claim: 'All things are delivered unto me of my Father and no man knoweth the Son but the Father.' Now let me try to reconstruct the whole situation. There is someone speaking. You look at Him and see He is a man. He is surrounded by a group of people who have attached themselves to Him, and who have been following Him and listening to His teaching. They have been with Him as He has travelled back and forth in the ancient land of Palestine. They have seen the works which He performed, and there He is, as it were, a man speaking to men. But when he says, 'All things', there is no limit to that word 'all'; it is as all-inclusive as a word can be. So who is this person who is speaking?

Let me tell you something about Him. He was born in a little place called Bethlehem. There was something strange and peculiar about His birth. His mother was not a married woman. She was betrothed to a man called Joseph, but not married, and she and Joseph had gone up together to Bethlehem to pay their taxes and have their name recorded in the census, because they happened to belong to 'the house and lineage of David', and the time of her delivery was at hand. You remember the old story. There were large numbers of people going to this little place and these two arrived somewhat late—apparently their journey had been delayed because of Mary's condition. Then they tried to find a place at the various inns and hostelries, but found that they were all full. No one would think for a moment of making room for them. They saw the woman and her condition, but life was much the same then as it is now, and those who had booked their rooms said, 'Why should I do anything? I have booked my room and paid my deposit; why should I move out?' It was the same selfishness that we all know so well, alas—every man for himself.

But there does seem to have been one man who had more compassion and kindness in his soul than the others. He could not take them into his inn but he did allow them to use his stable. So the baby was born in that stable and His crib was a manger. There is the child born into this world, and you remember how some shepherds came and told how they had heard a heavenly choir of angels who had told them to come to that very stable where they would see and hear wonderful things. Some wise men, too, came from a long distance to do their obeisance and to pay their homage to him. So there is the baby, exactly like every other baby to look at.

Then let us watch Him as He grows up into a little boy. There was something about Him that seemed unusual and extraordinary. He 'grew in favour with God and man'. When He was twelve, his mother Mary, and Joseph went to Jerusalem and He was with them; but when they were on their homeward journey, they suddenly missed Him and could not find Him. So they went back and found Him in the temple arguing with the learned doctors of the law, who put questions to Him which he could answer, and He was astonishing everybody. When Mary remonstrated with Him because He had not accompanied them, He replied, 'Wist ye not that I must be about my Father's business?'

Then there was a gap of eighteen years during which He spent His time working in Nazareth as a carpenter. But suddenly at the age of thirty He burst forth into His public ministry. He did certain things and the whole world was astounded. Even the doctors of the law were attracted at first, and they crowded round and listened to Him. There was something strange and wonderful about Him, something peculiar, something people could not fathom. They felt that while He was man like every other man, yet there was this mystery about Him.

So here He is, in these verses at this moment, speaking man to man, as it were, and this is what He says: 'All things are delivered unto me of my Father.' The one who was born in such utter poverty that they could not afford to bribe or to pay extra to get a bed; whose parents had no offering to offer when He was born save turtle doves; the one who was an artisan or an ordinary workman; who never went to the

schools or academies, and never had any special training;
there He is, a peasant from Galilee, and yet this is how He
speaks!

Let me summarise His astounding claim. He says first of
all that He is, in a unique sense, the Son of God—'*my* Father'.
He does not say 'of our Father'; He puts Himself into a
category apart, drawing a distinction between other people
and Himself. He did that very often. He said on another
occasion, 'I ascend unto my Father and your Father, and to
my God and your God' (Jn 20:17). He stands there as a man,
looking at men, and He pronounces to them this astounding
thing, that He is related to God in a way that no one else is—
'*my* Father'. John 5 has another more elaborate account,
probably of the same incident that we have here, and the Jews
were not slow to understand and realise what He meant. They
turned upon Him because He claimed God as His Father and
said that He claimed equality with God.

Now I feel that our real difficulty with the New Testament is that we are so familiar with these facts that we miss
their extraordinary character. Our whole danger, is it not, is
to fail to realise and remember that this is literal history. The
fact of Jesus Christ is history, and what I am calling your
attention to here is something that has actually happened.
This person was on earth and was born in Bethlehem; He
worked as a carpenter in Nazareth, and He told people that
He was the Son of God in a way that no one else was.

The second claim He makes is that He is, indeed, in a
unique relationship to God in the matter of His knowledge of
God. 'No man,' He says, 'knoweth the Son but the Father;
neither knoweth any man the Father save the Son.' In other
words, He looked at these people and said, 'You see me but
you do not really know me. The only one who really knows
me is God and I am the one, the only one, who really knows
God. You pray, you speak to God, but you do not know God
as I do.' We have been reminded that 'no man hath seen God
at any time', nor seen His shape. But He said that He had seen
Him and He claimed, as the Jews realised, an equality with

God the Father. He put Himself side by side with God. Occasionally He withdrew the veil and gave a glimpse of that eternal, mystical relationship between the Father and Himself, and He claimed that He was in such an intimate relationship with God that all men were outside it. Here He is, the carpenter of Nazareth, and yet that is what He claims.

But He claims even more than that! He says that He is in a unique relationship to this world: 'All things are delivered unto me of my Father.' He stands there and tells these people, 'Do you know that the whole of this world, the whole of time, the whole of history, heaven and earth and hell and all things, have been handed over to me by God the Father?' That is His claim: a unique sonship, a unique relationship to God and a unique relationship to this world. He stands there and says quietly that the whole world is in His hands. Never has the world seen or heard anyone who has claimed so much. Who is He, this babe of Bethlehem, this boy of Nazareth, this carpenter, this artisan, who claims that He is indeed the Son of God?

Well, let us approach the question by putting it, secondly, like this: why is it that people fail to recognise Him? For the fact is that those who were around and about Him, His own contemporaries, did not do so. They did not believe the claim, for had they done so, they would have submitted themselves to Him at once. As Paul wrote to the Corinthians, the princes of this world did not know him, 'for had they known him they would not have crucified the Lord of glory' (1 Cor 2:8). They did not know Him: they heard the claim but said, 'He is an imposter. Away with him, crucify him!'

Now I can understand someone saying, 'If what you state is true, if this person is the Son of God, well, why is it that the whole world does not believe on Him and go after and submit to Him?' Our Lord answers that question. 'No man,' He says, 'knoweth the Son.' What does He mean? Let me explain. We are concerned with the mystery of the incarnation and it is that which causes men to stumble. Let no one imagine that this is something simple. There is a mystery in the incarnation, there is a sense in which we can say quite honestly that had we been standing with that crowd when He was making this claim, we would have felt immediately and instinctively that there was something exaggerated. We would have felt that the claim that He was the one to whom all things had been committed; that He was the controller of the destinies of the universe; that all things had been put into His hands and under His power—that it was impossible. The whole mystery and marvel of the incarnation is involved at this point because He came in the likeness of sinful flesh. He did not come as a great king in the clouds of heaven, or with all the pomp of heaven around Him. No, He was born in that amazing way there in Bethlehem and His life was the kind of life I have been describing to you. There is this apparent contradiction. He was lowly of birth, taking on the form of a servant. He knew what it was to be tired. He suffered hunger and thirst. He was arrested in apparent weakness, and yet He said that all things were in His hands. But He did not even seem to be able to control a few soldiers, and He was nailed to a cross and died in utter weakness and shame and ignominy. That is why people found it difficult to believe His claim.

But the whole message of the New Testament is that when He came, He concealed His glory and emptied Himself. He divested Himself of the signs and insignia of His everlasting glory and Godhead and came in the form of a man and humbled Himself still more. The whole glory of the incarnation is in a sense its mystery, and as you read the Gospels, you will find that the two things are there constantly. He seems to be revealing and concealing at the same time. He shows forth His glory, yet hides it. He tells people not to tell anybody about His works, yet He upbraids them because they do not recognise Him as the result of His works. That is the cause of the difficulty, that in our Lord Himself there is an apparent contradiction. There is the almost apparent absurdity that this peasant of Galilee, this carpenter, should say, 'My Father,' and, 'All things are in my hands because God has given them to me.' It seems so incongruous; the everlasting and eternal

Deity, veiled in flesh, hid in human nature, and yet there. That is one reason why the whole world does not recognise Him and that is why He said to these people, 'You do not know me; you just see me as Jesus of Nazareth. Nobody knows me but my Father, the one with whom I have spent eternity; the one out of whose bosom I have come. You just see the external, you do not know the secret of it all, you cannot make a true judgement.'

The other reason for the failure to recognise Him is that we look at Him with our preconceived notions and ideas. We say that human greatness is always associated with pomp and external signs. Therefore, we argue, if God comes on earth, the signs will be still more wonderful and great, so that if the Son of God is come on earth, then any fool will be able to recognise Him. Not at all! It is just at that point that we go tragically astray. The Jews, alas, had their preconceived notions. Their idea of the coming Messiah was a great king, a mighty military power, one who would emancipate them from the thraldom and the yoke of their enemies and who would put them in the supreme position among all the nations in a political sense. Consequently, having such an idea in their minds of the Messiah, this peasant of Galilee, this carpenter, seemed to them almost a madman, He seemed so utterly ridiculous.

And today it is still the same. We so harbour our false notions of Christ and what He ought to do, that we do not recognise and believe that He has come. That is why the world has always asked this question as it has looked at Him: 'Who is this fellow, how has this man learning, having never learnt? Is not this the carpenter, the son of Joseph and Mary whom we know?' Indeed, those infinitely bigger and greater than ourselves have fallen into the same error. That incomparable preacher of Jesus Christ in later years, Paul, tells us in his autobiography, 'I verily thought within myself...' Why? Because he did not know Him; he had never seen Him; he just saw Jesus of Nazareth, a man among men. So Paul continues, 'I thought he was a blasphemer and I persecuted him and his way.' But, as we read in the book of Acts, as Paul went down to Damascus that afternoon his eyes were suddenly opened to the mystery. He now saw Jesus glorified, he saw Him with a veil of flesh removed, no longer a man. The glory of the Godhead was shining out and Paul fell to the ground blinded—he had come to know Him. God had revealed the Son to him, and he cried out to Him and said, 'Lord, what wilt thou have me to do?'

But again someone may ask, 'Well, if that is the case, why is there this mystery, all this concealing?' The New Testament provides the answer to that question in exactly the same way. I say it with reverence, the Son of God, when He came, had to come in that way and live and behave as He did, because it was the only way whereby He could save us. He cannot save us without identifying Himself with us. He even asked John the Baptist to baptise Him. He identifies Himself with us in our sin and degradation, and if He had come in the glory of the Godhead, it could never have been done. He had to conceal Himself, to divest Himself of it. He had to come in this way in the likeness of sinful flesh in order to become the Saviour, so the ignominy and the mystery and the marvel of His person were essential because of the work which He came to do. God forbid, therefore, that any of us should still stumble at the amazing mystery of the incarnation, the wondrous person of Jesus of Nazareth, the Son of God.

But, finally, what does His coming mean to us? Now here again our Lord puts it quite plainly for us in these extraordinary words: 'All things are delivered unto me of my Father.' What does He mean by that? Let me put it like this. What He says there can be put quite simply. He says that the world and its redemption has been handed over entirely to Him by God. He tells those people: 'I have come into this world. I have been sent by God, my Father, and He has given me a certain work to do. I am here to redeem this world and to hand it back, perfect, to the God against whom it has sinned.'

That is why Christ came. He tells us that He came into

this world in order that He might bear its sin. The punishment of sin is death—God had stated that in His ancient law. But the world has sinned, and if God should punish the sin of man, there would be no one left alive, everyone would be consigned to death and destruction. The Son has come to redeem the world, and here on earth He has taken upon Himself our sins and has borne the guilt and the punishment of sin in His own body on the cross. That is what He did when He was here; He made, and worked out, a way of redemption, a way of reconciling men and women to God.

What is He doing now? Well, as I understand the New Testament, He is now seated at the right hand of God in Heaven, where He is controlling the whole of this world and its destiny. History and time are in the hands of Jesus Christ, and ever since His ascension and entry into Heaven, He has been calling out a people to Himself. He is forming a new kingdom called the kingdom of God, and He is calling men and women out of this sinful world, which is doomed to destruction, and putting them into this new kingdom. It is a new kingdom with a new citizenship—it is growing, it is being built up.

Have you ever read church history with this idea controlling your mind? Do you not see them coming in twos and threes and sometimes in thousands down the running centuries? God is forming this mighty kingdom and the work is going on and on. 'All power,' said our Lord, 'has been given unto me in heaven and in earth. Go ye therefore, and teach all nations … and lo, I am with you always' (Mt 29:19–20). So the disciples carried out His command, and I do so also, for that is the business of preaching—calling out people for the new kingdom, and it will continue until that kingdom is completed. Then, He has told us, He will come back into this world and all those people who belong to His kingdom will be with Him; sin and evil will be judged and will be condemned and will be consigned to everlasting perdition. That is His statement, which He repeated many times.

History, therefore, is in the hands of Jesus of Nazareth,

this man who spoke. There is a definite end to time and history; He will come again, as a King this time, and there will be no mistake, no doubt. Every eye shall see Him, yes, and those who crucified Him, and they will know then what they have done. They will cry to the rocks to fall upon them and hide them from the wrath of the Lamb. That is what He is doing, and that is what He will do. He will wind up the affairs of this world one day. He will judge all wrong and sin and condemn it and consign it to perdition. Then, having removed all evil out of God's glorious work in creation, He will hand the kingdom back to His Father, and all who belong to it will spend eternity in His glorious presence and with the Father.

So I end on this note. What is the meaning of all this to us? What has the Son of God done to me by coming into this world, what difference has He made? Now it seems to me that there are certain inevitable deductions and here they are.

My relationship to God is determined solely and entirely and absolutely by Jesus Christ. If you tell me that you believe in God, I say to you that it is of no value if you do not believe in Christ. I say again with Martin Luther, 'I know of no God save Jesus Christ.' 'He that honoureth not the Son honoureth not the Father which hath sent him' (Jn 5:23); all things have been committed to Him. You cannot know God without Jesus Christ; 'No man knoweth the Father save the Son and he to whomsoever the Son will reveal him.' I cannot know God as my Father apart from Him. I have no forgiveness of sins if He, the Son of God, had not come and if He had not died for me on the cross. But because He has, I know my sins are forgiven. He and He alone can give me life anew; He imparts to me His own life and He makes me a child of God. He came to do that, and He has done it.

And lastly—and what a solemn thought—my eternal destiny is determined solely by my relationship to Him. I assure you in the name of God and of the Bible that when you come to the great Day of Judgement—for it is coming, we have all got to die and to meet God—I solemnly assure you that you will have only one question to answer. You will not be asked about the good you have done, or about your learning and knowledge, or your political party—none of these things will matter. There is only one question, which is: '*What think ye of Christ?* What do you make of my Son? I sent Him into the world and He came willingly. He was born a baby in Bethlehem and laid in a manger. He spoke, He worked His miracles, He died, and He rose again. He came and I handed it all over to Him, your redemption and salvation, and there on the cross He did His work. Have you believed on Him?'

It is our relationship to Jesus of Nazareth that determines and decides our everlasting and eternal destiny. God the Father has committed this world and all its affairs, my little life therefore included, to Him. But thank God He accepted the task! It meant suffering and scorn, it meant ignominy, it meant staggering up Golgotha, it meant nails being driven into His holy flesh. But at the end of it all He was able to cry out in triumph, 'It is finished!' He had accomplished the redemption and all who believe that and who believe in Him are eternally saved.

Beloved friends, do *you* know Him? Is Jesus of Nazareth to you the Son of God and the Saviour of your soul? The Lord of the universe? Make certain—your eternity depends upon it.

11

God's Good Pleasure

Even so Father, for so it seemed good in Thy sight (MATTHEW 11:26).

We are looking now at the twenty-sixth verse, the little verse that comes between these two other great statements. We have seen together how the incarnation happened in order that a great salvation might be available for you and for me, and for men and women in this world. There have been people who have believed on Him and who have found that that was the biggest and most important thing in their lives. If you look back and see the great story of the first confessors and martyrs, you see that there has been an unbroken succession of such people. There have been men and women who have gladly gone to the scaffold or the stake rather than deny Him. They have said to their persecutors that they know that in Him they have something that is bigger than anything else, and that if it is a question of renouncing Him or having the world, then they will reject the world and will risk their all upon Him. It is a glorious story. But, as we have seen, on the other hand there have been people who see nothing in all this and who dismiss it; and we have been considering together why this is so.

Now the trouble I feel with regard to all this, is always

the trouble with what we may call 'the approach'. It is about big principles that people go wrong. We spend a lot of time arguing about details, but it is with the main presuppositions that the real trouble tends to take place, and people stumble, as they have always done, at the very central message of the gospel itself.

So I want to look at that once more with you now. Our Lord here, in these words, stands aside, as it were, and looks at the great salvation which He Himself has come to bring and expresses His opinion concerning it. He marvels at it; He praises God for it, and He publicly acknowledges before the whole world how wonderful it is. He adds His testimony to it, for that is the meaning of 'I thank thee Father, Lord of heaven and earth.' He publicly acknowledges the perfection of God's scheme and plan of salvation. And here, therefore, is something which should help us to have a real grasp of the central purpose in this great salvation.

Let me put it like this—what is it that led to all that took place when the Son of God came into this world? We are all familiar with the facts, we have gone over them again and we know that it was all designed to work out this amazing plan. But what is it that has produced all this? What is at the back of God's unspeakable gift to this world and its people? And here, I think, we really have the answer. Now I wonder whether there is someone reading this who is still stumbling at the presuppositions on the approach to the gospel? Well, lest there be some such person, let us consider this great statement of our Lord together, because He tells us here of the source and origin of the salvation which He has come to bring.

He was, let me remind you, looking at the people, and He saw that some believed and that others did not. 'What is the explanation of this,' He said in effect to Himself. As we have seen, His reply was, 'I thank thee O Father, that thou hast hid these things from the wise and prudent and hast revealed them unto babes.' And the reason for this? 'Even so, Father, for so it seemed good in thy sight.' So let us look at these words. We can use alternative translations, in this way:

'Yes, Father for thus it was well pleasing before thee'—that
would do equally well; or, 'Even so Father, for such was thy
gracious will'—that is better; or take another: 'Even so
Father, for so was thy good pleasure, or thy good thought'; or
still another, 'Even so Father, for such was thy gracious
purpose.'

Now that, according to our Lord, is the explanation of it
all. He seems to be asking His Father, 'Why have I, thine
eternal Son, come into this world of time?' And that is the
answer: 'It was thy gracious purpose, thy gracious will.' He
traces it all back to that, and as you and I look out upon the
world and see it divided into Christian and non-Christian, we
see the explanation. It was God's gracious purpose for those
who believe the gospel, to believe it, and He calls them out. It
is the grace of God.

Let us divide that up in this way. This wonderful salvation of which we read in the New Testament, and which we
enjoy, is something that has been provided by God—that is
the first proposition. To be a Christian is not something that
is achieved by man; as we have seen, salvation is not something that people provide for themselves, it is something that
is provided by God for us. That is something which is absolutely basic and fundamental in the New Testament teaching.
In Ephesians 1 the Apostle Paul expresses it perhaps more
clearly than any other single portion of Scripture. He under-
lines and emphasises that particular aspect of this matter.
Notice how these words keep on recurring: 'according to the
purpose of his own will.' It is all of God's gracious purpose
and that, according to Paul, is the explanation of everything
that has taken place: 'Wherein he hath abounded toward us in
all wisdom and prudence, having made known unto us the
mystery of his will, according to his good pleasure which he
hath purposed in himself' (Eph 1:8–9). Read that first chapter
of Ephesians again and keep your eye on that expression and
you will find how the Apostle gives us that as the only
explanation. Of course, he is but paraphrasing what the angels
at our Lord's birth had already said: 'Glory to God in the

highest and on earth peace'—yes, but more than that—
'goodwill towards men' (Lk 2:14). That is the meaning of the
incarnation. A baby, the shepherds were told, has been born
in Bethlehem: 'Unto you hath been born this day in the city
of David a Saviour who is Christ the Lord.' Why has He
come? It is God's good will towards man—'according to the
good pleasure of His will', according to His own gracious
purpose.

Now we are so much the victims of sin that it is very
difficult for us to grasp that; we live in a world in which men
and women live by the sweat of their brow and by their own
wits. We live in a world in which we have to do things in
order to obtain results. Perhaps the commonest of all errors
with regard to the gospel is to regard salvation as something
which we work out for ourselves and which we achieve. That
is why people are always affirming their philosophies and
preparing their schemes and plans for renovation and
improvement and uplift and things of that kind. Yet the whole
beginning of the gospel and its message is that it is something
that is given; something that is sent and offered and handed to
us, something that is prepared by God.

Let me put it like this briefly. According to the teaching
of the New Testament, the Christian salvation was planned
before this world was ever made. Is that not what the Apostle
was telling the Ephesians? Furthermore, you will find it
everywhere in all his epistles. Before God made the world, He
had planned the way of salvation and of redemption. There in
eternity, a great eternal council took place, a council in which
were present the Father and the Son and the Holy Spirit. God
sees the end from the beginning. He saw the world which He
was going to make, and man, whom He was going to put
there and to whom He was going to give a free will. He knew
that man would sin and fall, and that therefore, a plan, a
scheme, of redemption would be essential. So the message is
that there in eternity, before time ever began, God planned
the whole of this redemption.

You and I have as little to do with it as that. Not only was our redemption planned and worked out by God before we were born; it was even perfected before the very world in which we live came into existence at all. Can I possibly put it more plainly than that? It is altogether from God, and we have as little to do with it as we have to do with receiving a gift. One of the great pleasures of Christmas or a birthday is the surprise which we get when someone brings us a gift. We do not know anything about it, they just spring a surprise upon us, and that is precisely what God has done. It all has its source, its fount, its origin in God's gracious will and purpose before time, away in eternity.

Let me go a step further and point out, secondly, that it is something which is entirely the result of His grace. Now the old theologians, those who lived before the middle of the nineteenth century, the truly Protestant reformed theologians, were very fond of teaching that God in creation revealed and manifested His power and that in providence He manifests His goodness, but that in salvation He manifests His grace—and what a wonderful word that is. It was the grace of God that sent the Son, and it was His grace that planned and schemed our redemption. Now grace, by definition, is 'unmerited favour'; it is doing something for someone who does not deserve it in any way. So the teaching of the New Testament about salvation is that it is something which is entirely generated in God. It is very difficult to grasp this great concept, and yet how important it is. The only explanation, says our Lord here, is, 'so it seemed good in thy sight'— such was thy gracious purpose, such was thy gracious will— and there is no other explanation. The grace of God is like a great fountain, self-generated in His holy being, not dependent upon anything else. If I may use such an expression, it has nothing to set it going, nothing to start it. It is independent of everything, but just the outpouring and the manifestation of His own glorious, gracious nature.

In other words, I would again emphasise that nothing led God to do this but God Himself. Nothing decided Him, for it was altogether in Him. Let me put it negatively. Salvation is not God's reward to man; it is not even God's response to man. So you see, it is at this point that all our human analogies and illustrations break down so hopelessly. I have used the illustration of our giving Christmas gifts to one another, and yet there is not a single instance or example of disinterested action because we are incapable of it. That is not being unkind to mankind, nor is it detracting from all the joy and pleasure of such things. It is just facing facts—we can never be disinterested. We love those who love us; we do not do these things indiscriminately to everybody—that is a general principle.

But when you come to God and salvation you are in an entirely different realm. It was not God looking down from heaven and, seeing man doing his best, saying, 'I must reward him by giving him salvation.' Not at all! 'God commendeth his love towards us in that while we were yet sinners Christ died for us' (Rom 5:8); or again, 'if *when we were enemies* we were reconciled unto God by the death of his Son'—that is it. So you see we have nothing to do with it, the amazing thing about Christian salvation is that it is altogether in spite of us.

Indeed, it is here we see the wonder of what God has done in Christ. God made the world, made it perfect, and put man into it. He had given man everything that man could possibly desire. Yet man in his folly rebelled against God and asserted his own self-centred will. Men and women thereby not only fell themselves and brought misery and ruin upon themselves, but they also marred God's perfect creation. What an insult to God; what an insult to this holy Father who had created the world and had treated them so generously! But that is what they did. They turned against God and began to hate Him. They became enemies of God and were alienated from Him.

That is what they have done as the result of sin and, therefore, they have deserved nothing but God's displeasure and hatred. They had been given everything, yet they spat in the face of God. They deserve punishment—they have broken the law and offended against that holy, loving gracious

Father. Yet the whole message of the gospel is just to say that in spite of all this, God made that great scheme of salvation. He sent it into the world even in the person of His only begotten Son, and all because of His own gracious nature, this fountain, this inexhaustible rising of grace within Him.

As you and I contemplate the message of Christian salvation in the Lord Jesus Christ, are we not driven back to the same words and to the same explanation as our Lord used—'Even so Father, for so it seemed good in thy sight.' As I realise that I, by nature, am a child of earth, born in sin, and have been a rebel against God, thinking of life as harsh and unkind; as I see that I have sinned in deed and in action and have had unworthy thoughts, I know that I deserve nothing but punishment to fit my crime. But when I look at the great salvation, I cannot explain it in any terms save these—it is all the result of the grace of God; I have done nothing to deserve it.

But let me remind you of what He has thus provided for us by His grace. I am never tired of repeating this great gospel. First, He has provided pardon, and that is a wonderful thing. Even though we have sinned wilfully and deliberately against Him, and though we have been guilty of the greatest sin of all, namely the hatred of His holy person, He forgives, and blots it out. We have pardon and free forgiveness without deserving it. Not only that, we are called back to Him and reconciled to Him. He smiles upon us and we have that adoption of children of which Paul wrote in the epistle to the Ephesians. Even though we are rebellious and have gone away, even though we have forfeited sonship, He gives us a new sonship, and takes us back into the family. Indeed, He regards us as fellow heirs with His only begotten Son and promises us eternal bliss at His own right hand. That is what the grace and the good pleasure of God has provided for us. Can we think of or imagine anything greater, or is there anything our whole tragic world needs more urgently than this?

We must also remember the way in which He did it. It was not by word, that was not enough—sin is such a problem and so terrible that words could not do it. He had to send His Son, who came and suffered and endured in this world in order that we might receive it. The cost of it all, let me repeat it again, was nothing but the gracious will of God. Oh, let us once and for ever get rid of this notion that it is in any way dependent upon us; that it is just a sort of beautiful gift of God because of mankind trying to scale the heights, mankind anxious to know and find Him. It is the exact opposite of that. It was as man was running away from God, that God came after him in his sin; it is all to be traced to His good pleasure.

So, then, I come to my last point. There is only one thing that you and I have to do with regard to this great salvation, which is to add our 'even so' or our 'yes'. Here is the Son of God contemplating it all. Look at Him as, in effect, He asks the question: 'Why all this'? See how He answers it and says, 'Yes Father—even so—for such was they gracious will.' And that is all that we have to do—just to say that. It is another way of saying we have but to receive the gift.

Let me analyse this a little. The only thing that we have to do is to recognise that this is the only way of salvation. This is why we preach it and with such urgency. For if God had not provided this way of salvation, we would all be lost, there is no other way. If God had not provided it, men and women would not be able to do anything about their lost estate and condition. We are all born in trespasses and sins, and we die in them and a corpse can do nothing.

People have been trying, ever since the Fall, to save themselves. You can read it not only in the Old Testament, but also in the best secular literature of the world. All philosophy is nothing but an attempt to achieve salvation. Men and women have always tried to do it, but they cannot. As Paul says, 'The world by wisdom knew not God' (1 Cor 1:21), and the world is unhappy because it is still trying to save itself and it never can. The greatest men and women the world has known have failed to save themselves and there is no greater folly than to try to do so.

If you are not convinced about that, then read the lives of

great Christians of the past and see how they tried to save themselves; how some of them forfeited great positions in this world and left society and segregated themselves not only from friends but from their families. They went into cells; they fasted; they sweated and prayed; they put on camel hair shirts; they said, 'Man must save himself, therefore if I am to save myself I must make myself absolutely holy. Nothing less than absolute perfection will do in the presence of God, and a man cannot do that in business or in a profession.' So they went out and became monks and hermits and lived in tents and caves and led their holy lives trying to save themselves. But in the end they realised how utterly impossible it was— we cannot save ourselves and try as we will, we can never succeed. Therefore, if God had not provided this way of salvation there would have been no way at all. So, as I hear the message of the gospel, I say, 'Yes, I thank you Lord, it is the only way.'

But I must also accept this way of salvation as it is. Now let us be quite clear about this. I say that there is no other way of salvation and then I am confronted by this offer of God in Jesus Christ. Does it not follow of necessity that I must take it and accept it as it is? To criticise this salvation or to question it is, it seems to me, the very essence of sin. Let me put it like this. Can you think of anything that is greater folly than to question or query it? Yet men and women do that. There they are, they are absolute beggars in a spiritual sense, and here dangling before them in the gospel are these amazing riches. But instead of accepting them and thanking God for them, they stand there in very great superiority and begin to examine and to question. They do not quite understand this, or they would not have put it like that. 'Surely,' they say, 'you do not tell us that we have all got to come to the penitent form as it were; that we can do nothing, and that we must all become babes. Ah yes, this sort of gospel is all right for the drunkard and for those in the gutter, but not for someone living a respectable life.'

So people proceed to criticise and examine. Out upon the

suggestion! We cannot save ourselves. We can be the best men
and women the world has ever known, but we are condemned
in the sight of God and His holy law. We may have amassed a
wealth of righteousness, but, 'that which is highly esteemed
among men,' said Christ, 'is abomination in the sight of God.'
Was there ever such folly as for a beggar to question and
criticise? Beggars cannot be choosers, and face to face with
God we are all paupers.

But I would also point out that this is not only sin and
folly. What base ingratitude it is, that people in their
arrogance should look at the gift of God and try to examine
and question and improve upon it. Men and women stumble
at this point. They say, 'Surely I must do my part.' No, the
first statement of the gospel is that you can do nothing—and
thank God you are not asked to do anything. Why is this hid
from the wise and prudent? Why has God revealed it unto
babes? All I know is that it was the Father's gracious pleasure
and purpose. Why have I a share in this? I have only one
answer: it was the grace of God that came to me.

If you are a Christian, examine your own experience.
Why are you what you are? Is it because of some special merit
that you possess? Can you honestly say, as you look back,
that it is because of something you have done or achieved?
No; must we not all say that were it not for the grace of God
we might be spending our days in all the foulness and the filth
and the godlessness of so much of the world—that might
have been our plight but for the grace of God.

Therefore, if all this is a gift from God, cannot you see
that you must accept it as it is? Do not try to understand at the
beginning; you will get to understand as you go on. Indeed
the more you go on, and the more you understand, the more
you will be amazed. I say, recognise your utter helplessness
and poverty, recognise your beggarly position and, instead of
asking your questions, receive, take hold of and accept it. In
other words, let me emphasise it again, the only thing we must
do is to take our stand by the Son of God Himself and join
Him in praising and in thanking God. As we have seen, that is

what He did. Here we see the man Jesus, as it were, looking back into that eternal council in which He had taken part when the great plan was evolved, and now on earth He pays His tribute to its wonder: 'Even so Father, for such was thy gracious purpose.'

And that is all that God asks and demands of us, that we look at this wondrous salvation which tells us that God did not spare His only begotten Son but sent Him into this world, even to death on the cross through which a way of forgiveness was made. He asks that we should realise that there He is offering us pardon and peace with Himself; a new life, a new beginning, a new outlook altogether, something beyond death and the grave that is indescribable and glorious, offering it us for nothing, as a free gift.

All He asks us is that we, likewise, should be ready to tell the whole world, if necessary, that we have seen it and accepted it; that we, ourselves, should confront our fellow men and women and say, 'Yes, even so Father, for so it seems good in thy sight'; 'according to his gracious purpose which he purposed in himself', the eternal will and wisdom of God combining with His love, mercy and compassion, and it all resulted in that first Christmas and everything that has come out of it. Have you uttered your 'Yes'? Have you, as you contemplate it, at last turned to God and said, 'Even so, Father, I see it is perfect, I cannot imagine anything better. I accept it and I receive it as it is.'

12

True Rest

Come unto me, all ye that labour and are heavy laden, and I will give you rest. Take my yoke upon you, and learn of me; for I am meek and lowly in heart: and ye shall find rest unto your souls. For my yoke is easy, and my burden is light (MATTHEW 11:28–30).

We are now going to consider together verse 28: 'Come unto me, all ye that labour and are heavy laden, and I will give you rest', but we must also look at the following two verses because they obviously complete the whole statement, and it would be false to the gospel itself just to take verse 28 without considering the others also. This great Christian salvation, about which we are concerned, is a life which has many facets, so it is essential that we should look at them occasionally one by one. Yet we must always remember the relationship of the parts to the whole and that is what makes it very difficult for anyone to preach on these three verses.

There are many difficulties about them. The first, and perhaps the greatest, is the very sublimity of the thought and of the language. There is a sense in which I always feel that it is almost wrong to preach on these verses at all. One feels that no one should say or do anything to detract from the magnificence and the glory of the thought and of the whole conception. This is by no means the first time I have attempted to preach on these three verses, but I have never come anywhere near satisfying myself hitherto in all my efforts and attempts, and I am quite sure that I shall feel precisely the same now. Indeed I can go further; with all the sermons I have ever heard or read on these extraordinary verses, I have felt that somehow or another they always baffle us because of their greatness and their glory. And yet it behoves us to consider them and to look at them.

Another difficulty is the comprehensiveness of the statement. So much is said here in a few words; indeed the whole compass of Christian doctrine is, in a sense, to be found in these verses, which makes it difficult for anyone to analyse them because, of necessity, we cannot state the whole of the doctrine in so brief a space. I have the feeling somehow that if one could only say these words as they should be said, that that would be more than enough in and of itself. But as we cannot do that, then let us look at them, let us make certain observations concerning them, and let us, by the grace of God and the guidance of the Holy Spirit, trust that something of the inner meaning and glory of these gracious words may come, not only to our minds but to our very hearts, and move us as we have never been moved before. Certainly nothing more gracious, more wonderful, is to be found even in the pages of the four Gospels than these words which were uttered by our Lord at this point, and there is a sense in which one feels that graciousness and glory all the more as one takes the words in their context.

Let me remind you of that context. We have been working our way through this eleventh chapter of Matthew. We have seen how, at the very beginning, John sent his messengers to our Lord saying, 'Art thou he that should come or look we for another?', and how our Lord realised that in one way or another people will persist in stumbling at Him. Then we have considered how our Lord dealt with these things and spoke to the people, and as we went along we came across some very harsh words: 'Woe to thee Chorazin.' He had lived and worked in these cities, but the people had missed their opportunity. It is the end, He said—'Woe unto you'—and that is here in the context. Then you remember how, having pronounced these words, our Lord, as it were, turned from the world back to His Father and uttered the sublime words found in verses 25–27. There, as we saw, is very high doctrine; knowledge is given to some and withheld from others.

And now our Lord, having considered all the hindrances and obstacles, and having spoken to the Father about it, turns back to the people and says, 'Come unto me all ye that labour and are heavy laden, and I will give you rest.' Thank God that we have such words! Thank God that in this modern world I can take a text like this. Thank God that with things as they are at this moment we have something like this to turn to. Thank God, too, that when so much is falling around and about us, He still remains and continues to speak the same gracious words.

The world we live in is ill and tired, and most of us are feeling old and weary. I am reminded of the lines once written by G.K. Chesterton to a friend: 'The world was very old indeed when you and I were young.' He meant by this that he knew something of the ancient character and the tiredness of life and of the world, and that perhaps is one of the main problems of life at this present time. We look around us and we see little to comfort, little to cheer, little to give us hope. There is a feeling abroad among some people that the world really is entering into a state of senile decay. Men and women tend to believe the message of Scripture and are beginning to ask whether we really are facing the end of all things, the end of time and the end of history. We have exerted ourselves so much that we can exert ourselves no more.

But thank God that into such a world come these words of our Lord's. They are an invitation that seems to include us, which speaks to us exactly as we are and where we are and exactly as we feel. Thank God, too, that it is not just another command and cloak of austerity, for that is what the world is doing to us today. It is using the lash of its whip, and we are all tired. We are asked for still further exertion, we are always being called to endure something more or to attempt something more. But thank God that here we have an offer, a gift, and not some violent exhortation to still more impossible effort.

So let me try to summarise this great message by putting it to you in the form of some three or four propositions. I think they are perfectly obvious and self-evident, but, unfortunately, most of our troubles in this world today are due to the fact that we will not look at and recognise the obvious. It is the things that are self-evident that are being forgotten. We are very subtle, very clever, that is one of the great characteristics of our age. We have sophisticated devices with which we can split the atom, yet we ignore first principles. Therefore, what we need above everything else is to have another look at the self-evident and obvious.

Let me put it like this. The greatest need of the world and of mankind is just rest. I have been saying that we are tired, and, as tired people always are, we are restless. It is a curious psychological point that this should be so, but these things go together and it is true also of the world. There is nothing so obvious here as a lack of ease, a lack of quiet. One of our words at the present time is 'hectic'. Life has indeed become hectic when we compare it with say 100 years or even 50 years ago. You cannot but be impressed by the terrible restlessness. We are all so busy; we work shorter hours, yet we have lost time. We have mechanical devices that ought to save us a lot of time, yet we are all saying we have not got any time. It is this strange restlessness, this loss of ease and poise and balance which you see in every realm and department of life. You cannot pick up a newspaper but you see it shouting at you. International discord, international problems, everything seems uncertain, and we seem to be sitting on a volcano, or as a ship on the ocean being tossed about. Everyone wonders what the outcome will be.

But it is not confined, alas, to nations and to the international condition. You get it in groups, inside the different groups within the nation itself. People seem to be unable to settle down. They do not seem to be happy, there is something wrong somewhere. Then there is trouble and discord and misunderstanding running right through life, not only politically but industrially and socially and even in the family realm. This is to be seen everywhere. We hear about the restlessness of youth, but everybody is restless. People are not as placid as they used to be; men and women are ill at ease, and they are unhappy.

Now most of life today can only be understood when we view it from that particular standpoint. That is to me the only explanation of the so-called pleasure mania. People were never so intent on pleasure as they are today. Look at the drink bill, the gambling, the amount of money being spent on entertainment—never has more money been spent on sheer pleasure than at the present time. It is this restlessness once again. That is why I try never to denounce people who are victims of the pleasure mania, for to do so is almost like denouncing someone who has a physical illness. They are to be pitied, and above all by Christian people and by the Christian church. Men and women are buying these pleasures and spending their money and giving their time and energy to these things for one reason only, and that is that they cannot face life without them. They are unhappy, they are facing something they do not like, so they are rushing away from it.

All the upsets in life are due to this same restlessness. All the terrible increases in separations and divorces are ultimately to be brought back to this: men and women feel that somehow or another if only they take this step they will find happiness and rest, but then they find they have not got what they thought they were going to get and so they try further experiments. Still they do not find it and on and on it goes, one experiment after another. I was reading a local paper from a certain part of the country the other day and there I saw a perfect instance of this very thing, how the body of a poor woman and that of a little child had been found in the river. She had left the usual note about being fed up with life,

and at the inquest it was stated that she was a married woman
living away from her husband, living with another married
man. She had broken her vows and pledges and she had said,
'If only … then I will find it.' But she had not found it, and
that is the sort of thing that can be multiplied by thousands. It
is nothing but this tragic, pathetic restlessness that has come
to be the most prominent characteristic of the world at the
present time, this desire to find rest and peace and some kind
of tranquillity.

Now this restlessness, if we analyse it, manifests itself in
certain realms in particular. There is the restlessness in the
conscience, and that is why we are doing so much to get away
from ourselves. If we spend time with ourselves, or talk to and
examine ourselves, we will soon begin to feel unhappy. Our
conscience condemns us; we have a bad conscience and a bad
conscience makes us restless. We want to get away from it, to
forget it.

It is exactly the same in the realm of the mind and
thought. We are all face to face with such tremendous problems; the problems of history and of time, and the problem of
the world and of its future. It is not surprising, therefore, that
there is an intellectual restlessness at the present time. If we
had lived in the mid-Victorian era we should not have known
that particular problem. They felt then that at last they had
solved these issues and they were settling down. We talk
about the halcyon days of the mid-Victorian period. They
thought that man had come into his own, but the philosophies
of those times have been made to look rather silly by the two
major world wars of this century and the things that happened
in between, and, too, by the things that are still happening.
The whole problem is back with us again, and so there is an
intellectual restlessness.

There is restlessness also in the realm of the heart and of
the desire. We are longing for something we cannot find.
There is something within us that is crying out for satisfaction, but the world does not seem to be able to give it to us. So
as a result of all these things the greatest need of mankind is
for rest.

And that in turn brings me to the second proposition, which is that that rest is only to be found in a knowledge of God. Our Lord had just been talking about that before He gave His invitation. Let me remind you of those preceding verses: 'I thank thee O Father, Lord of heaven and earth because thou hast hid these things from the wise and prudent and hast revealed them unto babes. Even so Father for so it seemed good in thy sight. All things are delivered unto me of my Father and no man knoweth the Son but the Father, neither knoweth any man the Father save the Son and he to whomsoever the Son willeth to reveal him.' Then He says, 'Come unto me, all ye that labour and are heavy laden, and I will give you rest.' In other words our Lord is saying, 'In this very knowledge that I alone have of the Father—that is the secret of rest'; and that is the connection between these verses and those that precede.

Or let me put it like this. Every other kind of rest that man has or has not achieved is nothing but a false rest. Now I grant readily that there is a false sense of rest, and one of the first things that a preacher has to do is to show people that sometimes they are resting in that. There are certain people, for instance, who may come and say, 'I am not interested in Christ's invitation, but I am at rest.' Yes, but so many of them are in a state of rest for one reason only, which is that they will not face the problems, and that is quite possible. We have often seen a child do that. When children have been reprimanded for doing something that is wrong, they do not like it and they become unhappy. So they conjure up a world of their own and turn their back upon the parent who has given the reprimand. They play with their toys, and there in this wonderful little world of their own they persuade themselves that they are perfectly happy.

There are many adult people who are doing that. They will not face the facts. They refuse to look at life, or to think deliberately, putting a cloak over anything in them which stimulates thought. There are others who try to achieve rest in any way they can. Some do it by drugging themselves. I have already referred to this in some of the illustrations I have given. There are many ways in which we can drug ourselves and drugs can give a false sense of rest. Isn't that the whole trouble with the opium addict? He feels restless and ill at ease so he takes his opium pipe and smokes it, or he gives himself an injection of morphia. And then, for a time, he feels completely happy and everything is perfect in the world. The man has achieved a kind of rest, but is it really rest? No, it is just one variety of artificial rest of which the mind is capable. There are many ways of taking drugs. Pleasure is just a drug and there are thousands of people in the world today who say they are not interested in the gospel and its message because, as a result of drugging themselves, they have achieved some measure of a false sense of peace.

Then there are others who do exactly the same thing by just creating a world of fancy and of fantasy for themselves. We are strange creatures and we play psychological tricks with ourselves as well as with one another. There are people who deliberately act a part and thus they go through life looking at themselves and deliberately playing this part they have created for themselves. But they, too, are evading the problems.

I designate all these things as illustrations of false rest because whenever you come to the great crises and questions of life you discover very quickly how utterly false they all are. When you face a drastic illness, or when you face sorrow or bereavement, or when you find yourself on your death bed, then you have to face it. You cannot go on fooling or drugging yourself. Your money ends, or something you have done suddenly collapses, or there are the inevitabilities of life, and then all the things I have outlined do not help you. That is where suicide comes in. People know they have got to face a certain thing but they cannot, and that means that they are failures. We can go on deceiving ourselves for a long time, but eventually we have to face it and that is why it seems to me that people who do not face the gospel are not only in a tragic position, they are fools. We know that the end must come,

and when it does, none of these things are going to be of any
avail to us. All those other matters are but false, and sooner or
later they will let us down.

But the gospel announces that rest is only to be found in
a knowledge of God, because God has made us and He has
made us in such a way that we never can know rest apart from
Him. The great Augustine of Hippo put that perfectly when
he said, 'Thou hast made us for thyself and our souls are
restless until they find their rest in thee.' You can scale the
heights or plumb the depths, you can travel round the world,
as many people have done, trying to find rest and peace, but
you will never find it. God has so made us—and this is the
glory and the dignity of man—that nothing can finally be
made at rest until our souls are satisfied in God. And the
world, I suggest to you, is an eloquent sermon on that particular theme. With all that we have in the modern world of
wealth and culture and education and everything else, look at
the picture of unutterable restlessness all around us. 'There is
no peace, saith my God, to the wicked.' There is no rest apart
from a knowledge of God.

That leads me to my third proposition, which is that our
Lord alone can give us this knowledge. 'Come unto me, all ye
that labour and are heavy laden, and I will give you rest. Take
my yoke upon you and learn of me.' Notice the personal
reference; all along He is pointing to Himself. Yes, but He is
doing more than that; He is contrasting Himself with everybody else. His claim is that 'no man knoweth the Father save
the Son and he to whomsoever the Son willeth to reveal him'.
He says that not only can He give us this knowledge of God,
but that no one and nothing else can give us and create this
knowledge in us.

And you see how He puts it: 'Come unto me, all ye that
labour and are heavy laden.' Now these two words are interesting. The picture He conjures up is that of a labouring
person, someone who is restless. They have come to see that
what they really need is a knowledge of God, and so they set
out to try to find Him. They try this way and that, making

this effort and that attempt. A classic illustration of one of these 'labouring' people is Martin Luther before his conversion. Look at that monk; he has left the world, and has taken up what is called a religious vocation. He has left family and friends, and there he is in his cell, fasting, sweating, praying, counting his beads, all in an attempt to find God. Look at the labour of it all, as he tries to make himself good enough to stand in the presence of God. There is no harder labour in the world than an effort and an endeavour to find God.

But this is what happens to those who try to do that. They become weary and tired in this endless work, because the more they read their Bible and the more they try to live the good life and to find God, the more they discover their own sinfulness and the absolute, unutterable holiness of God, and on and on they go. But those who come to God in Christ are those who are tired and restless; such are the labouring class referred to by our Lord, people who have set out on the spiritual quest of a knowledge of God.

Yes, but not only that, he also refers to those who are heavy laden. What does that mean? I can put it like this. If you try to find God yourself and, having failed, you turn to others and ask them how to find Him; if you have become aware of this restlessness in life, and have come to see that nothing can satisfy you but a knowledge of God and you ask how you can obtain this knowledge, then someone may say to you, 'Well you must start reading philosophy. God is ultimate and absolute, and you have to start considering the whole question of being itself, the ultimate essence.' So they put the burden of philosophy upon your back and you have to try to understand these things. It does not matter if you have had no education; 'That is the way,' they say, 'You must delve into the mysteries!'

Then you go to another who says, 'No, that is not the way. Rather, you must take up the mystic quest. In a sense, the whole art of finding God is *not* to think; indeed to stop thinking. You must make yourself a blank, and pass through the dark night of the soul. You must relax, become absolutely passive, and forget yourself.' Have you ever tried it? What a burden that is, to tell people to lose or to forget themselves—that is another burden that is put on your back.

Then the third is the moral burden. 'God is good,' some people say, 'and He is holy. So if you want to know Him, you must start to live a new life.' So you turn over a new leaf. You start with your New Year's resolutions; you read the Bible, the Ten Commandments and the Sermon on the Mount, then you set out to live that life, believing that unless you do you will never know God.

Are not those the ways that are recommended to us when we say that we want to find God and to know Him? We have already been labouring and those are the burdens that they put upon us. 'Come unto me,' says Christ, 'all ye that labour and are heavy laden.' The people to whom He spoke had known something of all that I have been describing. They knew the Pharisees, with their 614 points of the law, those religious leaders of whom our Lord said, 'You put burdens on these people that you cannot carry yourselves.' As the Apostle Peter put it at the Council of Jerusalem in the time of the early Church, this yoke was too much, no man could stand it (Acts 15:10). Such are the burdens that the world would put upon us when we say that we would know God and speak to Him and find rest for our souls. No, it is Christ alone that can do it and He can truly give us rest.

How does He do it? This is the great message of the gospel. Christ gives us rest by answering all the problems and the questions that I have already put to you. I want rest within, and I want rest in the world that is outside me—Christ alone can give me rest within. I need it, too, in the realm of my conscience. I look back across the past months; is everything there perfectly in accord with what I desired? Am I happy as I review my life? Is there anyone who has done nothing of which he or she is ashamed? No, our conscience condemns and accuses us. How can I get rid of my past; how can I erase the blots and get rid of my guilt and sin? Can philosophy help me, can moral effort and striving, can mysticism, can any of these things? No, they do not touch my problem. There is only one whom I know can do this, and it is the one who issues the gracious invitation. He has borne my sins in His own body on the cross. They have been dealt with by God in Him, and as I look at the cross of Calvary, I find rest to my conscience. I know the debt has been paid, the penalty has been suffered, my sin has been blotted out, and there God forgives me.

And likewise, He gives rest to my mind. I want to know God, and I hear Him say, 'He that hath seen me hath seen the Father also. Look at me and you see the Father; look at me and take of me if you would know God.' In the gospel, I find satisfaction to my mind that I find nowhere else. It is here alone I feel I am in direct contact with ultimate realities and absolute truth. There is no problem of my life but that the gospel deals with it and answers it. I find intellectual rest and an answer to all my questions.

And, thank God, my heart and my desires are also satisfied. I find complete satisfaction in Christ. There is no desire, there is nothing that my heart can crave for but He can more than satisfy. All the restlessness of desire is quelled by Him as He breathes His peace into my troubles and problems and restlessness.

But He also gives me rest and peace in my environment and in the world that is around and about me. How important this is at the present time, as we look at the world and its prospects. For though I may have rest and peace within me there are things outside me that disturb me—how can I still maintain rest in such a troubled world? Here again, Christ alone can answer my problem, for the gospel prepares me for these things. It is the gospel that has prophesied the kind of world in which we find ourselves. It was the philosophers and politicians who promised us a perfect world in the twentieth century. But the gospel of Christ promised the exact opposite, so long as man sinned against God. It is here alone that I understand this modern world. Though wars and pestilences may come, and though the whole world may be rocking at its very foundation, I have here a view of life which tells me that in spite of it all, the Lord God omnipotent reigneth. I know that this Christ, who once uttered these gracious words, who was here on earth and who died and rose again and ascended into heaven and is seated at the right hand of the Father waiting until His enemies shall be made His footstool, I know that He will come back, and that the world of sin and evil will be routed and destroyed. There will be a new heaven and a new earth 'wherein dwelleth righteousness', and all who have accepted Him will be with Him there and will reign with Him and share His glory for ever.

So I am given rest in spite of my circumstances. The gospel enables me to say with the Apostle Paul, 'I am persuaded'—which means, I am certain—'that neither death nor life nor angels, nor principalities, nor powers, nor things present nor things to come, Nor height, nor depth, nor any other creature shall be able to separate us from the love of God, which is in Christ Jesus our Lord' (Rom 8:38–39). That is perfect rest which is independent of circumstances; that is to be calm in the midst of storm:

> Peace, perfect peace, in this dark world of sin?
> The blood of Jesus whispers peace within.
>
> E.H. Bickersteth

That, then, is His invitation, and still He sends out the same word. 'Come unto me.' Oh look at Him! Have you ever seen anyone like Him? Can you explain Him except in terms that He is the only begotten Son of God? Look at His miracles; look at what He did in those three hurried years of His public ministry; look at Him! He is the one who calls you, and who can offer you rest, because He is the only one who has ever been in this world who knew perfect rest Himself. Look at Him from His birth to His death. In spite of all He suffered and endured, there was always peace; even in the garden of Gethsemane, He was at peace; even on the cross, he said, 'Father into thy hand I commit my Spirit.'

He knew rest, and He calls you to come to Him. He gave

this rest to many in the days of His flesh, and He has continued to give it ever since. Saul of Tarsus was a very restless man, breathing out threatenings and hatred, but He met him and gave him rest. Our Lord invites all to come: 'Come unto me *all* ye that labour and are heavy laden.' If you are labouring, if you are heavy laden, come! The invitation is for you wherever you are, whatever you may be. Thank God, too, He tells us that He is meek and lowly. I do not find the modern philosophers to be like that. I listen to them and their terms and their cleverness and art, but I cannot follow them. 'Come unto me,' says Christ. 'I am meek and lowly and you shall find rest for your souls.'

Oh blessed invitation! Oh blessed word that comes to all that labour and are heavy laden; to those who are unhappy in life, those who feel restless, those who have not found satisfaction. Come to Him, speak to Him, tell Him about yourself and your condition. Surrender yourself to Him, listen to Him, and He will give you rest.

13

The Yoke of Christ

Come unto me, all ye that labour and are heavy laden, and I will give you rest. Take my yoke upon you, and learn of me; for I am meek and lowly in heart: and ye shall find rest unto your souls. For my yoke is easy, and my burden is light (MATTHEW 11:28–30).

We have seen that it is Christ and He alone who can give us true rest, and this is something which has been verified so often in the long history of the Christian church. Indeed, if you read the biographies of all the most notable saints which the church has ever known, you will find that this is the common element in all their experience. They all tell you that they had been seeking God; they had become aware of a sense of dissatisfaction within them; they were unhappy and ill at ease, and they had all come to see that the ultimate need was the need for God Himself. So they had set out to seek God, and they tell us, many of them, in their autobiographies, of their painful way and of their searching. Read the life of Augustine, and you will see it there, how he was labouring and heavy laden; read it in the story of Martin Luther, and of John Calvin; read it, too, in the lives of John Wesley and his brother Charles. It does not matter which you take, it is a repetition of this self-same thing. Here were men seeking rest and peace, labouring and trying to find God, and all who offered them help just imposed fresh burdens and loads upon their tired shoulders. And then they go on to tell us how sometimes suddenly, sometimes gradually—it does not matter which—they at long last found it, and found it in Jesus Christ. They found rest and peace; they found all that they had been attempting to find with no benefit and no result; all the fruitless effort and striving had in a sense been quite unnecessary; until suddenly or gradually they saw that it was a gift that has to be received and accepted; and receiving it they found rest to their souls.

Now that is the position as it confronts us today. Here in this gospel is the very thing we need, whatever the nature of our problem. So why is it that men and women, with such a wonderful possibility and such a wonderful offer, nevertheless still go on struggling and striving and labouring and sweating, still knowing the same restlessness and dissatisfaction? What is the trouble? Well, the particular difficulty I want to deal with now is that of the type of person who, hearing all that I have said, turns to me and says something like this: 'Yes, that is all right, but what I want to know is what exactly is meant by "coming to Christ". You say that this is the most gracious invitation the world has ever heard or can hear. You say it is as simple as that. All I have to do is to come to Christ, and if I do I shall find rest for my weary soul.'

'Why', says this person, 'that is the one thing I want above everything else, but my trouble is that I don't know what that phrase means. It is an evangelical expression which I have heard many times but what does it mean in actual practice? What must I do—I want that peace, how am I to obtain it?'

Now I want to try to show you that our Lord Himself has already answered that question in the invitation. We concentrated in the last chapter on verse 28, now I want to put the emphasis on verse 29. I would say again that the statement must always be taken as a whole. There is a sense in which you cannot divide it, and yet for the sake of emphasis, it is perhaps not only legitimate but also important that we should consider the different verses separately. How do I come to Christ? Here is the answer, 'Take my yoke upon you, and learn of me; for I am meek and lowly in heart: and ye shall find rest unto your souls.'

So let us look at that and divide it up—the first thing that coming to Christ means is, take the yoke of Christ upon us. 'Wait a minute,' says someone, 'there again is a phrase that sounds all right as a phrase, but what exactly does that, too, mean?' Now I am trying at this point to be simple and practical. I have made a great statement about the gospel, and now I am really concerned with the mechanics, if we can use such an expression, of actually coming to Christ. I recognise very readily that these are the things that often hinder men and women from knowing the peace and rest which the gospel has to give. I recognise the danger of men like myself standing in a pulpit and using phrases which do not carry the same meaning to the listener as they do perhaps to me. What, then, does Christ mean when He invites us to take His yoke upon us?

Well, another way of putting it is that we must become attached to Him as our teacher. The idea of the yoke is a familiar one, and it was especially familiar to those people to whom our Lord was speaking. If you have a picture in your mind, therefore, of a pair of oxen yoked together and pulling a plough, you have the main essential of this particular expression. This had become the illustration that was often used in connection with learning and teaching. If you attached yourself to a particular teacher it was said that you had become yoked to that teacher, or you had come under his yoke, and it is a very good expression. So the first thing our Lord tells us is that if we want to know his peace, the first thing we must do is to decide quite deliberately to listen to Him and to His teaching.

Now here we are in this world and we are concerned about these matters. We have been thinking, we are not just drugging ourselves. We are aware of the fact that life is a big and serious matter and we are dissatisfied. We have come to see that the real problem is that of knowing God. So we want to know Him and find Him, and immediately we are confronted by quite a variety of different teachings. Never perhaps was that more true than it is at the present time.

It was true, of course, when our Lord was here in the flesh on earth. Just think of the people of Palestine. There were many teachers offering ways of life to them; there were the Pharisees, the Scribes and the Sadducees. Greek philosophy, too, was beginning to penetrate. There were travelling philosophers in that ancient world, everyone of whom claimed that he had the answer to the problem of life. Take that picture which we have in Acts 17 of the life of a typical Greek city with its various temples to the different gods; and in these temples there were always teachers. The ancient world was remarkably like our own. It was a kind of Speakers' Corner, with its various men telling them what they needed. And it is exactly the same today; the world is a glorified Hyde Park with people setting forth their views and ideas.

But what our Lord tells us can be put as simply and plainly as this—if you want to know rest and peace, the first thing you must decide is to forsake all the other teachings and teachers and to listen to Him. It is as simple as that. Again, I could prove that by quoting the cases of many of these great men in the history of the church to whom I have already referred. Take a man like John Wesley. There he was, a learned man, a man who was essentially a scholar. He had gone to Oxford; he was a fellow of his College, and was obviously a man who had read many books and who enjoyed doing so—it was part of his calling. But later in his life he said that he had become 'a man of one Book.'

Now there is a sense in which we all have to arrive at that particular point. I have to say to myself in this matter, I must shut myself up to this one Book, the Bible, this one revelation, because you cannot be yoked to many people at the same time. A yoke, in a sense, only takes two—the teacher and yourself—so if you are going to be yoked to Christ you must get rid of the other teachers, the exponents of other views. 'You have been listening to these others,' says our Lord in effect to the people, 'to these Pharisees and Scribes and Doctors of the law and what have they given you? Have they given you rest and peace? Have you found the satisfaction that you desire? Have they done anything to you except to put these additional loads and burdens on your shoulders which have almost crushed you to the ground? Come out of that yoke, be yoked to me; "Take my yoke upon you and learn of me."'

But let me take it even a step further and put it like this. It means that at the very beginning we must recognise this person, Jesus Christ. Having considered all these matters I say to myself, 'Well, I have failed; these other things do not help me. Here I see this man, who claims to be the Son of God. Very well, I will go to Him and I will listen to what He has to say.' That is taking His yoke upon you. Let me put it still more practically. It means I decide that I become, to use the language of the Lord Himself, as a little child. How often He said that! 'Except ye be converted and become as little children, ye shall not enter into the kingdom of heaven.'

He put it in different language to that ruler, Nicodemus. 'Now Nicodemus, stop!' He says, in effect. 'You are starting the wrong way, you are coming as an examiner. You must come as a child, you must come to receive and listen; take my yoke upon you.' The difficulty for many of us has been, has it not, that we come to the Bible and to Jesus Christ as critics. *We* are the examiners. We do not come and sit at His feet and look up into His face and listen. Rather, we come full of our own theories and ideas. We say, 'No, we do not quite understand this, we want an explanation of that.' Christ is turned into a sort of pupil who is going to be examined by us. We are the authorities and He is, as it were, being tested.

But that is not taking His yoke upon us, and let me assure you solemnly of this fact before I go any further. As long as you stand in confidence upon your own feet to criticise the

Son of God and His gospel, you will never know rest. It is only those who come weary and heavy laden and who drop on their knees and say, 'God the Son, speak to me!' They are the only people who ever find this blessed rest. You have to come as suppliants, forsaking all others and your own wisdom and understanding. You must acknowledge and confess that all the teaching of the world has not given you rest. No, you come to Him and say, 'Speak to me, I am here to listen. I have come as a little child.' And once more, if you go through the whole range of Christian biography, you will find it has always been like that. They have at last come to see Him. They have become tired of it all, and have gone to Him as little children. That is taking His yoke upon us. It means that our very approach is of vital importance, because there is one way only to come, and if we do not come that way we will never know the blessedness of it.

But, secondly, if being yoked to Christ means that, then 'learning' of Christ follows in a very logical sequence. Learning of Him means that having taken His yoke, we now wait to listen to what He says. We believe what He says and accept it. So what has He to say to us? Let me once more summarise the salient statements of this blessed gospel. In effect our Lord was saying to these people, 'Now the Pharisees have told you what you have to do; they have told you to wash the outside of the cup and platter; they have their 640 rules and regulations; they pay tithes of mint and anise and cummin and they have added burden upon burden ... But now, listen to me, learn of me.'

His teaching presents us with an entire contrast to everything the world has to tell us. He taught us the holiness of God, and always emphasised it. You go to the other teachers and they tell you that God is love. They tell you, 'Everything is all right, don't listen to that puritanical type of preaching.' But when the disciples came to our Lord and said, 'Lord, teach us to pray as John also taught his disciples,' He replied, 'When ye pray say, "Our Father which art in heaven, *Hallowed by thy name*"' (Lk 11:1–2). You must start, said our

Lord, with a right conception of God. Now is this not where we all tend to go astray? So often our initial error and trouble is that our ideas of God are so loose. Let us be quite frank and honest about this. Most of us, before we listen to Jesus Christ, rather feel that we are in a position even to criticise God: 'Why should God? Why this? Why that?' We are still the judges even where God is concerned. Now what our Lord tells us at the beginning is this, 'Put off thy shoes from off thy feet, for the place whereon thou standest is holy ground' (Ex 3:5). Can you imagine God, can you picture Him? God is utterly and absolutely holy, so much so that we cannot imagine Him, eternal in His holiness and His absolute perfection.

That is what our Lord taught about God, and we must start there. We have to realise that if to know God is the first essential thing in rest and peace, we must begin by knowing something of His nature and character, and that is what our Lord always taught about Him. Take His own attitude towards the Father. Look at the time He spent in prayer; observe the way in which He was always careful to say He did nothing of Himself; that the works which He did were those the Father had given Him to do, and that all the words He spoke were those that the Father gave Him. Observe His subservience to the Father, the respect with which He spoke of Him. 'Learn of me,' said our Lord, and it is only as we listen to Him that we can have any true conception of God, as regards His holiness and love and every other quality and attribute that is in Him.

But what was His teaching about us? He tells us about our sinfulness. Those other teachers, He told the people, would have you believe that it is what goes into the mouth that defiles a man, and that is why you are surrounded by rules and regulations. But I say to you, 'Not that which goeth into the mouth defileth a man; ... but those things which proceed out of the mouth come forth from the heart; and they defile the man. For out of the heart proceed evil thoughts, murders, adulteries, fornications, thefts, false witness, blasphemies: These are the things which defile a man' (Mt 15:11,

18–20). The heart is polluted and sinful and unworthy—that is His teaching about us.

But look by contrast at the modern popular philosophies. They will never tell you that. They will tell you that the troubles are not due to you, but to other people. They teach that the whole trouble with us is that we are never given a chance. They are defending and sheltering us all the time. But if we are going to listen to Christ, we will know that it is our own hearts that really are the cause of the trouble. He tells us that our hearts are so vile that we need clean, new hearts; we need to be born again. He tells us that we are so sunk in sin that nothing but His coming into this world could possibly deliver us from it. Furthermore, before you know the rest and peace which Christ has to give, you are going to be made very restless and unhappy—this is one of the steps through which you must pass. He always condemns before He saves, He always knocks down before He lifts up, He always exposes the ill before He applies the cure. You will never know salvation and conversion without passing through conviction. If we do not know what is meant by being convicted of our sinfulness, we have not heard His word. No one ever comes truly to Christ without being made to see himself as a wretched, vile and condemned sinner, and listening to Christ brings us to that realisation.

Then let me emphasise what He tells us about our own position, which is that as we are, without Him, we are all under the wrath of God. He taught that God is the Judge eternal. He stated very plainly that when we die we all have to stand face to face with God in the judgement, and He taught that every man stands condemned before God: 'God so loved the world that he gave his only begotten Son that whosoever believeth on him should not perish but have everlasting life. ... He that believeth on him is not condemned,' yes, 'but he that believeth not is condemned already because he hath not believed in the name of the only begotten Son of God' (Jn 3:16,18). Later on in that chapter it is put like this: 'the wrath of God abideth on him' (Jn 3:36).

'But,' says someone, 'I do not believe in that God of yours, who is an angry God. I do not believe in the wrath of God, I am too enlightened.' Well, my friend, there you have gone out of the yoke of Christ, and are listening to modern teachers. I say that to come under His yoke is to sit and listen to Him, and is what He taught. You talk about the love of God, but He is the incarnation of the love of God, for in Him is the love of God dwelling in all its fullness. There was never such love as that, and yet those are the very words that He used. It was He, of all people, who tells us that as we are by nature, and that apart from Him, we are all condemned sinners in the sight of God.

He once put that perfectly in painting His picture of the Pharisee and the publican who went up into the temple to pray. When the Pharisee prayed, he thanked God that he was not as other people, especially this sort of publican. 'I fast twice in the week, I give tithes of all that I possess.' How wonderful he was! The other man, by contrast, 'would not lift up so much as his eyes unto heaven.' He just cried out, saying, 'God be merciful to me a sinner.' Yet that is the man 'who went down to his house justified', the man who realised that he was an utter abject sinner in the sight of God and who cast himself upon God's mercy (Lk 18:9–14).

So our Lord teaches us about the holiness of God and our own sinfulness. Then, thirdly, He teaches that there is only one way of escape from the wrath of God, which is that we must listen to what He says. He says, 'The Son of man is come to seek and to save that which is lost' (Lk 19:10), and, 'The Son of man came not to be ministered unto but to minister and to give his life a ransom for many' (Mk 10:45). To put it another way, the Lord Jesus Christ is telling us, 'I have come into this world for one reason only, and that is to save you. You cannot save yourselves; no one else can save you. God gave you the law, but you cannot keep it. He sent His prophets but you would not respond to their message. Greek philosophy has already been in this world for 300 years and more, and yet it does not come to a knowledge of God. I, the Son of Man, am come to seek and to save that which is lost. "Except a corn of wheat fall into the ground and die it abideth alone; but if it die it bringeth forth much fruit.... And I, if I be lifted up from the earth will draw all men unto me."'—'This he said, signifying what death he should die'—(Jn 12:24,32–33). 'Take my yoke upon you and learn of me.' So as I listen to Him I learn that He tells me He has come into this world to die for me and my sin. The punishment of sin is death, so if sin is punished in me, I am dead and outside the life of God, and I remain in everlasting misery and restlessness. But He tells me that He has come to bear my sin, to die my death and to reconcile me to God.

The next thing He tells me is, as we have seen, that before I can realise all this, I must be born again. As He told Nicodemus, 'Except a man be born again he cannot see the kingdom of God.... Ye must be born again' (Jn 3:3,7). Our Lord taught that and He went on repeating it. He said, in effect, 'Look, here I am unlike every other teacher who has come before you. I am not exhorting you to do something, for that is putting a further load on your shoulders. I am come that you might have life, and have it more abundantly.' He taught that we need the life of God and He said that He had come to give it—regeneration and rebirth, a new nature, a new start, a new beginning, a new creation.

And then the final element in His teaching is that He calls upon us who have believed all this to deny ourselves, to take up the cross and to follow Him. Whoever believes that is someone who is prepared to risk anything, even to be considered a fool. That is taking up your cross—to say no to yourself and everything in yourself that makes you say that you cannot do such a thing. It does not matter what they say, you deliberately take up your cross and follow Him. You may be despised by the world, as He was, and laughed at as He was. Indeed, you will be crucified spiritually and in many sensitive ways which will hurt you—it may even cost you your life. But those who really listen to Him will gladly do it. So live the Christian life, set out to follow His example, and try to live the Sermon on the Mount where He has portrayed the Christian life. Having believed all the rest, take His yoke upon you and learn of Him.

And then, briefly, the final step. Having listened to Him and heard Him say all that, the final step in coming to Christ is just this: that having come under His yoke, having been convicted and convinced of the truth of what He tells me, in utter simplicity I just tell Him that I believe it. Yes, it means telling Him in words; it means that in utter simplicity you get down on your knees and just tell God that you believe what the Lord Jesus Christ has taught you. You tell God, in words, that you realise now that you have sinned against Him, that you have had unworthy thoughts about Him, and have said unworthy things about Him, you tell Him that you have ventured in your arrogance to criticise Him, that you trusted to yourself that as you were you were fit to stand in His holy presence—and that, perhaps, was the greatest insult of all, to think that you were good enough for that.

Confess it all in words with utter shame. Tell Him you have now come to see quite clearly that if you lived for a thousand years you could never make yourself fit to meet Him, and therefore you acknowledge that you are an utter sinner, and that you deserve His wrath and condemnation. Tell him, too, that you have heard this word of Christ and that you have believed it; that you do believe that Jesus of Nazareth was His only begotten Son and that you have heard Him saying that He has come to bear your sins and to die your death. Tell Him you believe that, that you are resting upon it. Ask God to make it plain to you. You still may not understand, but whether you do or not, you believe in utter simplicity. It has to come to that, we all have to be humbled. The greatest intellects have to get right down and see that they are as helpless as anyone else and have just got to believe simply that the Son of God has died for them and that that is the only way of forgiveness.

So you tell God that in words and then you thank Him for it, you thank Him for sending His Son, you thank Him for His patience and long suffering, and then you tell Him that you want to commit your life to Him and to surrender yourself to Him. You say that your one desire is to please Him; that He has loved you in such an amazing way, He has done so much for you that you realise He has a right to the whole of your life and you tell Him that you want to give it to Him and to go after Christ. You tell Him, then you get up and set about doing it. You tell men and women that you believe this and accept it and then you practise the Christian life. You look to Him for strength and power and guidance; you align yourself with God's people; you hear His word as often as you can; you pray to Him without ceasing; you read the Bible, you become a man or woman of one Book and you spend your time with this. You do all you can to know Him better and better, that thereby you may express your gratitude and thanksgiving and your praise to Him.

That is what coming to Christ means. Listen to His word, accept it and in simplicity act upon it. You will not understand everything, but you just commit yourself to Him and you go on asking the Holy Spirit to give you more and more light and knowledge. Then you practise the knowledge you are given increasingly, but continue to ask for more, and you will go on experiencing the rest for your soul and the peace and the joy of God which the world can neither give nor ever take away.

Beloved friend, have you come to Christ? He still calls today, 'Come unto me, all ye that labour and are heavy laden, and I will give you rest.' You have not found it without Him—that is certain—and you never will. So come in utter simplicity, take His yoke upon you and learn of Him and you shall find rest unto your souls.

14

The Free Gift

*Come unto me, all ye that labour and are heavy laden, and I
will give you rest. Take my yoke upon you, and learn of me;
for I am meek and lowly in heart: and ye shall find rest unto
your souls. For my yoke is easy, and my burden is light*
(MATTHEW 11:28–30).

As we look for the third time at these three great verses,
it seems to me that there is still one other matter left
which we have to consider. I have been emphasising
all along that this statement is a whole, and must always be
taken as such, and yet it is so comprehensive a statement of
the gospel that no man can do justice to it in one discourse. As
we have seen, it divides itself up into the three verses. We
started with the invitation 'Come unto me all ye that labour
and are heavy laden, and I will give you rest.' Then we looked
at what it means to 'Take my yoke upon you and learn of me;
for I am meek and lowly of heart: and ye shall find rest unto
your souls.' And now we turn to 'For my yoke is easy and my
burden is light.' Now there, I think, we are introduced to
what is, perhaps, in the last analysis, the thing that more
than anything else tends to stand between men and women
and the acceptance of this gracious invitation; and, therefore,
between them and the experience in their actual daily life and

practice of the blessings of salvation through this glorious gospel.

I feel increasingly that the fundamental difficulty with so many is in the whole matter of their approach to the gospel. They start with such an initial misconception of the very nature of the Christian life that they really are unable to travel even a single step in the direction of truly coming to Christ. People will persist in regarding the gospel as if it were but one among a number of teachings. You see this constantly in books and journals and articles. People have got into the way of talking glibly about Moses, Isaiah, Jesus, Paul, Plato, Socrates, Gandhi and others. So the Lord is put in a series with others and then, of course, His teaching is just one of a number of philosophies with respect to life.

That initial misconception is fatal, and it is because we approach it in that way that we constantly ask our questions and continue to have our difficulties and problems, our perplexities and misunderstandings. People seem to come to it with this attitude of common sense and say, 'Whenever I am confronted by a teaching which offers to help me in this world and life, I come to it and apply my mind to it. I ask my questions and I want to have them answered.' So they come like that to the gospel of Jesus Christ and there, from the very beginning, they are doing something that as long as it persists is going to make it quite impossible for them truly to know this gospel and what it has to give. Our Lord has said that already: 'I thank thee O Father, Lord of heaven and earth, because thou hast hid these things from the wise and prudent, and hast revealed them unto babes. Even so, Father, for so it seemed good in thy sight.'

But now I am anxious to put that in this particular way. The first thing we must realise as we even approach this matter is that the gospel is altogether different. Everything we have been accustomed to in every other realm must here be put on one side. When we enter the house of God to consider His word, we must realise that everything that may be true of us outside ceases to be true here. Outside, of course, we differ very much. Some have ability, others lack it. Some have knowledge and learning and culture and understanding; others are illiterate, and, of course, outside the church all that is very important. If you are going to listen to an address on philosophy you must have ability and understanding; there must be something in you that is capable of receiving what is said to you. If you listen to a political address you must know something of the elements, at any rate, of the things that the speaker is talking about. The same applies to an address on art or music or literature. They all make demands upon us, and according to our differing abilities so will be our possibility of receiving them.

But that is no longer the case when you come face to face with the gospel of Jesus Christ. Thank God, here is something that is altogether, utterly different. Our very approach must be different, so our mentality and our outlook and attitude must not conform to what we have always been accustomed to. We must come in a new way.

The New Testament is full of this. Take our Lord Himself who, as we saw earlier, put it like this: 'Except ye be converted and become as little children ye shall in no wise enter into the kingdom of heaven.' We all have to come to a common denominator and become as little children, whatever we may be naturally outside. 'Ye must,' He said, 'be born again.' These are His statements; we must have a new beginning—it is altogether different. So we can put it like this. We are here, quite definitely, in the realm of the miraculous and the supernatural—that is the great initial postulate.

In other words, far from apologising for the miraculous element in the gospel, I assert it, and the tragedy of the last 100 years is that the church has apologised for it. She has tried to hide it and has given the impression that the gospel is just a sort of moral teaching with improvements. However, the New Testament gives the lie direct to all that, and we start with the position that the gospel of Jesus Christ is in a category of its own. It is not a philosophy, nor is it human teaching; it is miraculous, it is supernatural. It is not man reaching out to God, but God reaching out to man, so that we start on an entirely different level and our very presuppositions must be changed. And that is the difficulty at which so many people still continue to stumble.

Let us be quite clear about this however. I am not suggesting that the gospel is therefore irrational, nor am I simply proclaiming that because it is miraculous and supernatural it is therefore unreasonable. Not at all! What I am saying is that we are here entering a realm which we cannot enter by reason alone. It is not unreasonable but it transcends our reason. It is advanced reason if you like, a higher reason. It is not unreasonable for me to believe that when God acts, I cannot understand Him; and that is precisely what we are confronted with when we come to the gospel of the Lord Jesus Christ.

Let no one imagine, therefore, that the teaching is that we just leave our intellects outside when we come into the house of God and abandon ourselves in a passive state to any feeling that may come, or to any kind of emotion. Far from it! But we do say that when God does something, we must accept it as being supernatural and miraculous, and we must not, therefore, be surprised when we find that it is so.

We must believe and accept what God has done and then proceed to understand. To me the argument comes in this way. As a human being in this world I have been conscious of the need of rest. I have used my mind and my reason; I have listened to the world and its teaching and all its philosophies, but I find that they cannot give me rest and I am at the end of my tether. Then I am here confronted with a new offer which says, 'Listen to this.' I say it is reasonable to listen, and the moment I do so I begin to find that what He has to say is indeed essentially different.

Now I want to show you something of the miraculous and supernatural nature of the gospel as our Lord Himself shows it in these three verses. He says a number of things here, and if you just look at them on the surface, you may very well come to the conclusion that it is just a series of self-contradictions; it seems quite unreasonable and almost ridiculous to the natural man. Look at it like this. Here is one who stands before us and says, 'Come unto me ... and I will give you rest.' He has already mentioned certain things about Himself: 'All things are delivered unto me of my Father: and no man knoweth the Son, but the Father; neither knoweth any man the Father, save the Son, and he to whomsoever the Son will reveal him.' He is claiming He is God—the carpenter of Nazareth! He is a man standing among men and yet He does not hesitate to say, 'Come unto me,' or, in effect, 'Where the world has failed you, I have a unique knowledge of God and I give you a knowledge of God that no one else can.' He puts Himself above all others, and yet the next moment He is saying, 'I am meek and lowly in heart'—it is one of those beautiful paradoxes about Him, at one moment exalting and at the next moment abasing Himself, God, man, and the two natures at the same time.

So we are confronted by that—'Learn of me, take my yoke upon you'—the demand for totalitarian allegiance which He constantly made. There was a man called Matthew sitting at the receipt of custom and our Lord said to him, 'Follow me!' and he immediately followed Him. There were two men attending to the nets and boats of their father and He said to them, 'Follow me,' and they too went after Him. He demands this allegiance and yet He says, 'I am meek and lowly in heart.' Can you understand Him? Are all your human categories of any value here? Are all the yardsticks by which you measure mankind outside the Christian church of any value at this point? How do you explain and expound Him? Here is something that baffles at the very beginning, the wonderful invitation seems to be a contradiction to us.

But observe the same thing in regard to His teaching. It is certainly the most exalted teaching that mankind has ever known. You can put together all the teaching of all the great teachers throughout world history and then compare them with that of the Lord Jesus Christ and you will find that it stands above them all. It is above the law, the Ten Commandments and the moral law that were given to the children of

Israel through Moses, the prophet of God. Take all the exalted, ethical teachings of mankind; look at them and then compare them with that of the Lord Jesus Christ and you will find that if they are difficult, then His is surely impossible. The people, he says, who will be blessed are those who are 'poor in spirit'; 'they that hunger and thirst after righteousness shall be filled'; and 'the pure in heart shall see God' (Mt 5:3,6,8).

'Except,' He says, 'your righteousness shall exceed the righteousness of the scribes and Pharisees ye shall in no case enter into the kingdom of heaven' (Mt 5:20). 'Be ye therefore perfect even as your Father which is in heaven is perfect' (Mt 5:48). 'Bless them that curse you, do good to them that hate you, and pray for them which despitefully use you and persecute you' (Mt 5:44). Then, 'If any man will sue thee at the law and take away thy coat, let him have thy cloke also. And whosoever shall compel thee to go a mile go with him twain' (Mt 5:40–41). 'Love your enemies'—that is His teaching.

He also said, 'If any man say he will come after me, let him deny himself, and take up his cross and follow me. For whosoever will save his life shall lose it and whosoever will lose his life for my sake shall find it' or save it (Mt 16:24–24,25). Then, as we saw in the last chapter, He said that it is not that which goes into the mouth that defiles people but that which comes out of the mouth, out of the heart. He says that what we must do is cleanse our hearts and purify our minds.

Then you remember His conversation with the so-called rich young ruler? He was an excellent young man. He honoured his father and mother, he gave a tenth of his goods to feed the poor, he was almost a paragon of all the virtues, and yet our Lord looked into the face of such a man—who shames us and makes us feel unworthy—and said, 'One thing thou lackest.' That is the kind of teaching which we find from Him, that is what He tells us, and then He looks at us and says, 'My yoke is easy and my burden is light.'

You see the essential paradox of His teaching? Does He not seem to be contradicting Himself once more, even as He did in His own person—as He was God and man and as He was exalted and abased? And here we have it again, the most impossible teaching mankind has ever known, and yet 'My yoke is easy and my burden is light.' 'Ah,' says someone, 'that is why I cannot understand your gospel; that is why I am not a Christian. You claim that there is a gracious invitation, "Come unto me", but the kind of life you offer is too difficult—where is the rest and the peace?'

Then let us look at the extraordinary paradox that He paints even with regard to us. The people whom He invites are those who are already tired out. We are labouring and heavy laden, conscious of failure and of a desperate sense of need. We listen to Him as He expounds this extraordinary teaching of His, and the paradox is that He offers us rest, though we deny ourselves, take up the cross and follow Him who was never convicted of sin and at whom no one could ever point a finger. He says we can have peace and rest even as we follow Him, and, still more marvellous, He offers us this immediately. This is the miracle of the gospel; this rest is offered to us here and now, not after a course of treatment and training. Indeed, 'Take my yoke upon you,' He says, 'and learn of me' and you will find still more rest for your souls, yes, have it, and you will get more. That is what He offers to us, tired, weary, forlorn, bruised and battered by life—and He offers it without any delay.

Furthermore, it is an offer which is made to all: 'Come unto me *all* ye....' It does not matter what your antecedents have been; the gospel is not interested in your family history. It does not want to know about your past record and about the examinations you have passed or failed. The gospel of Jesus Christ only asks you one thing. Do you need rest? Have you failed to find it; are you desperately in need of it? Well, if so, come!

There, then, are some of these extraordinary things that we find at once, and we have not even begun to look at the gospel yet. So how do we reconcile these apparent paradoxes and bring them together? Well, I have already answered the question at the very beginning. The real answer to all this is that it is none other than the whole nature of the gospel. It sounds different and it *is* different; and it is different because it is miraculous and because it is supernatural. Let me explain. The Lord Jesus Christ Himself, the speaker, is unique. He stands alone. He is not just a man; He is not only a teacher, or just another philosopher; He is not still another idea as to how life is to be lived that we may find peace.

No, He is the Son of God—God and man in one peson—so you see, we are in a different realm. We very rightly closely examine and scrutinise men who come to us and offer us their panaceas and wonderful solutions for the problems of life. We are naturally sceptical—and it is the essence of wisdom to be sceptical in a world like this. We have met such people before and we have known that their philosophies and teachings lead to nothing. We find that these men are even sceptical themselves. We have the long history of the world behind us, and in it we read how men have come and advocated brilliant ideas all of which have led to nothing.

But here we start with a different person, someone who cannot come into our human categories. He is not man like everybody else. He was 'made in the likeness of sinful flesh', but only *in the likeness*. He is the one who has come into this world from the outside, the Son of God incarnate. We start by proclaiming the miracle of the virgin birth and the incarnation, for if Jesus of Nazareth was not born in that manner, I have no gospel. He is unique. It was about Him and Him alone that the voice from heaven said, 'This is my beloved Son in whom I am well pleased' (Mt 3:17). So I suggest to you that you will never resolve the apparent paradox of Jesus of Nazareth until you have come to know that He is indeed the Son of God. You will never be happy about all this apparent contradiction of what He said and did until, with Thomas of old, you humble yourself and say, 'My Lord and my God.' But the moment you say that you will understand Him—and not until then.

But let us go on and look at the second aspect of this

matter: if that is the person, what was the purpose of His coming? Here again we have the clear and explicit answer of the New Testament gospel. The Lord Jesus Christ came into this world not simply to teach, not just to exhort us, not simply to encourage us in our hopeless quest for God and not just to give us a pattern and example. Let me explode that fallacy once and for ever, and I can do so very simply. For, if Jesus of Nazareth is nothing but a pattern and example to me and an encourager, then, I say it with reverence, I wish He had never come. When I look at the teaching of the Old Testament, at some of the Patriarchs, at a man like David and some of the prophets, I feel I am left hopelessly behind. When I look at some of the best people the world has ever known, I am humbled and humiliated as I compare my puny efforts with theirs. So are you going to ask me to believe that I have to follow this other person, this Jesus of Nazareth? Is He just going to give me an example? I say I am undone if that is the case, because He condemns me before I take a single step. It is impossible!

But, thank God, He did not come to do that! He came into this world not just to give a fillip to our efforts, not merely to goad and urge us on, because that would be adding to the load and the burden which is already weighing heavily upon our shoulders. No, He came into this world to do something for us; He came to do a work which was none other than to work out the way of salvation for us. So He came 'in the likeness of sinful flesh' and took upon Him human nature in order that He might take upon Himself the problem of our sins and their guilt. And He did it; He went to the cross and there He died, and the result is that He confronts us with an offer.

So the greatest word that He uses here is one which includes the whole gospel; it is the word 'give': 'Come unto me all ye that are weary and heavy laden and I will'—outline the way of life to you? Tell you of greater heights you have to scale? Go ahead and as you see me you will imitate my example? Not at all! 'Come unto me all ye that labour and are heavy laden and I will *give*'—I will hand over to you, I will impart to you. The gospel of the Lord Jesus Christ is one that gives, and it is the only thing in the world which does that. All other teachings make demands. They demand more learning, more intellect, more understanding, more moral effort, more striving.

But our Lord gives us a gift, a free gift. Here is summed up the very essence of the gospel of Jesus Christ and all that you and I have to do is to realise our need. We are not asked to achieve anything at the beginning, we are just asked to receive.

Our Lord put it perfectly on another occasion when He said, 'Ask and it shall be given you; seek and ye shall find; knock and it shall be opened unto you' (Mt 7:7). In other words, 'If you realise that you are a pauper, that you are a failure, ask and I will give.' The whole gospel is here: 'God so loved the world that he gave his only begotten Son, that whosoever believeth in him should not perish.' This is the gospel of God and all that is postulated of us is that we realise our need.

Finally, what is it that He gives us? How does He give us this rest? Well, the thing we need first of all is forgiveness. I stand confronted with my own past life and its failure and its sin, and I can do nothing about it. I cannot get rid of it. I may try to forget it, but it is when I am taken ill or loved ones are taken ill or when I see an open grave that I realise that it is always with me, and when I think of death it comes back. The haunting finger of the past with all my misdeeds is there. My first need is forgiveness and I am restless because I need it. Then He looks at me and says, 'Come unto me and I will give you rest'; the rest of forgiveness, the rest of peace with God. As the Apostle Paul says, 'Therefore being justified by faith we have peace with God' (Rom 5:1); and, 'There is, therefore, now no condemnation to them which are in Christ Jesus' (Rom 8:1). You find rest from this whole matter of your past sinfulness and guilt. He has dealt with it, He has borne it, so He can give you rest. But He does not stop at that. He also gives us a new life and nature. This, of course, is the most astounding thing of all—the doctrine of rebirth—which is why I made the emphasis I did at the beginning, for before you can understand this gospel you must have a new life. 'Ye must be born again'; that is what He said even to someone like Nicodemus, who was such an excellent man, a master in Israel, and such a moral person. He says, 'My friend you want new life, a new nature and without it you will understand nothing'; and that is exactly what He gives me.

'Now,' says someone, 'you are beginning to talk to me personally because my problem has always been that I do not understand these things. It sounds too good to be true, just too wonderful. You say we may have rest and peace at once, but the world isn't like that. Everything I have obtained in life has been as the result of a struggle and effort and striving, so how can these things be?'

His answer is that if you come to Him genuinely and truly and in sincerity, He wil give you a new nature. You will have a new mind and a new understanding. You will desire different things and you will hate the things you used to desire—my friend, this gospel is a miracle! It is not a moral teaching only, nor a moral striving. The Lord Jesus Christ offers to give us His own nature. You can become like Him and you will not know yourself. You will say with Paul, 'I live; yet not I but Christ liveth in me' (Gal 2:20); that is the gospel. He will give you the rest that comes with a new nature, and a rebirth, and an entirely new outlook with respect to life.

And He promises likewise to give us the Holy Spirit, and it is with the Holy Spirit that we receive power and strength to live this life that Christ outlines to us. That is the ultimate explanation of this extraordinary statement that His yoke is easy and His burden is light. 'But,' someone may ask, 'He preached the Sermon on the Mount, and that applies to Christian people today. How can I live it?' Here is His answer: 'I will give you the power in the Holy Spirit, I will enable you to live the Sermon on the Mount.' So He asks us to follow His blessed and glorious example and enables us to do it; He does not leave us to ourselves. That, again, is where the miraculous and the supernatural element enters into this gospel. He does not make a demand of us until He has given us the life and the power that are requisite to the performance. He Himself enters into us, saying, 'I will give you another Comforter. I shall be in you, dwelling within you.' He will live His own life in us and enable us to live that life, so His yoke is easy and His burden is light.

All that is not mere theory. Read the lives and biographies of the saints and they will all tell you the same thing. They will tell you that before they knew Christ, they were failures in life. They could not keep their own standards, and they could not satisfy the moral demands of men. But once they had come to know Christ, they could, with ease, live a life infinitely greater and more difficult. Because He is with us in the yoke, He is there sharing the burden with us. We became yoked to Him and He, the great burden-bearer himself, bears the weight so that we run, as it were, by His side.

That, my friend, is the explanation of the paradox. You can only understand Him and His death, and the Christian life, by realising that He offers to give life itself, the life of God. The divine life becomes ours, He is in us, transforming and changing us and enabling us to do the impossible.

That is His offer, and even now He stands unseen and makes the offer again. 'Come unto me all ye that labour and are heavy laden, and I will give you rest. Take my yoke upon you and learn of me for I am meek and lowly in heart and ye shall find rest unto your souls. For my yoke is easy and my burden is light.'

Have you received this life divine? Are you a new creature, a new person? What is your idea of Christianity—striving frantically to be a Christian or receiving the gift of life from Christ? That is His offer. We receive new life first as a gift and then we practise it in the power of His might and of His strength. Have you life anew? Do you know you are a child of God? Can you say, with Paul, 'Abba Father'? Are you aware that the Spirit of Christ is in you? 'If any man have not the Spirit of Christ,' says Paul, 'he is none of his.' To be a Christian means that you are aware of another within you, a new nature. If you have it, thank God! If you have not got it, it is my privilege to tell you once more that all you have to do is to tell Him in words that you have not got it and that you would like to receive it. Ask Him for it, and He Himself has said, 'Him that cometh unto me I will in no wise cast out.'